Gun Violence and
Mass Shootings

Bradley Steffens

About the Author

Bradley Steffens is a poet, a novelist, and an award-winning author of more than forty nonfiction books for children and young adults. He is a two-time recipient of the San Diego Book Award for Best Young Adult and Children's Nonfiction: His *Giants* won the 2005 award, and his *J.K. Rowling* claimed the 2007 prize. Steffens also received the Theodor S. Geisel Award for best book by a San Diego County author in 2007.

© 2019 ReferencePoint Press, Inc.
Printed in the United States

For more information, contact:
ReferencePoint Press, Inc.
PO Box 27779
San Diego, CA 92198
www.ReferencePointPress.com

LIBRARY OF CONGRESS CATALOGING-IN-PUBLICATION DATA

Name: Steffens, Bradley, 1955– author.
Title: Gun Violence and Mass Shootings/by Bradley Steffens.
Description: San Diego, CA: ReferencePoint Press, Inc., 2019. | Includes
    bibliographical references. | Audience: Grade 9–12.
Identifiers: LCCN 2018018183 (print) | LCCN 2018030619 (ebook) | ISBN
    9781682825167 (eBook) | ISBN 9781682825150 | ISBN 9781682825150 (hardback)
Subjects: LCSH: Gun control—United States—Juvenile literature. | Mass
    shootings—United States—Juvenile literature. | Violent crimes—United
    States—Juvenile literature. | Firearms ownership—Government
    policy—United States—Juvenile literature. | School shootings—United
    States—Juvenile literature.
Classification: LCC HV7436 (ebook) | LCC HV7436 .S75 2019 (print) | DDC
    363.330973—dc23
LC record available at https://lccn.loc.gov/2018018183

Contents

Introduction

Parkland and Beyond

At 2:19 p.m. on Wednesday, February 14, 2018, an Uber driver dropped off nineteen-year-old Nikolas Cruz outside Marjory Stoneman Douglas High School (MSD) in Parkland, Florida. With the school day drawing to a close, the campus gates were unlocked. Cruz, a former MSD student, knew they would be. He walked through the gate, crossed the campus, and entered Building 12, a three-story structure with thirty-three classrooms. On the second floor, Cruz opened a black case containing an AR-15 rifle and began to load it. Freshman Chris McKenna came across Cruz in the hallway. "You'd better get out of here," Cruz told McKenna. "Things are gonna start getting messy."[1]

McKenna ran for help, and moments later Cruz began shooting into classrooms and at anyone who appeared in the hallways. Some students fled the building. Others hid in their classrooms. Teachers called 911. Students texted their parents. Cruz moved from floor to floor, shooting. An armed sheriff's deputy took up a position outside the building, but he did not enter. Alerted by McKenna, football coach Aaron Feis ran to Building 12 and started directing students to safety. Cruz gunned him down. As police arrived, Cruz dropped his gun and melted into the crowd of fleeing students. Fourteen students and three teachers lay dead. Sixteen others were injured. The shooting lasted only seven minutes, but its effects would be felt by the survivors and the victims' families for the rest of their lives.

A Plague of Violence

Horrific as it was, Parkland was not the worst mass shooting in US history. Less than five months earlier, a gunman in Las Vegas had opened fire on a crowd of concertgoers at the Route 91 Harvest music festival, killing fifty-eight people and injuring more than eight hundred. According to the *Washington Post*, there have been 150 mass shootings since 1966. These attacks have claimed 1,077 lives. Twenty-one of these shootings took place at schools and colleges, leaving 194 dead.

While the carnage from mass shootings is horrifying, mass shooting deaths make up a tiny percentage of the gun-related deaths that occur the United States each year. In 2017 the ninety-four mass shooting deaths made up less than three-tenths of 1 percent of the more than thirty thousand total gun deaths that year. As *New York Times* columnist Nicholas Kristof pointed out in 2015, "More Americans have died from guns in the United States since 1968 than on battlefields of all the wars in American history."[2] The most recent figures show that there have been more than 1,516,000 gun-related deaths in the United States since 1968. That compares to 1,396,733 Americans who have died in all of the nation's military conflicts, from the Revolutionary War to the Global War on Terrorism through 2017.

> "More Americans have died from guns in the United States since 1968 than on battlefields of all the wars in American history."[2]
>
> —Nicholas Kristof, columnist for the *New York Times*

Although the number of school shooting deaths is relatively small, their emotional impact is great. School shootings tend to attract more attention than other shootings do because of the ages of the victims and the sheer senselessness of the attacks. "A student's obituary should not contain the phrase 'Gunned down while studying for a chemistry test,'"[3] writes Kathy Durham, a social studies teacher at West Wendover High School in West Wendover, Nevada.

New Voices for New Policies

As is often the case after a mass shooting, outraged citizens called on the authorities to reduce gun violence. The aftermath of the Parkland shooting was different, however, because that time it was the student survivors, more than teachers, parents, or politicians, who were calling for change. And they were not simply requesting it. They were demanding it. "Your job is to protect us,"[4] MSD student Cameron Kasky told his senator, Marco Rubio, on the CBS News program *Face the Nation*. "I don't want your condolences," MSD junior Sarah Chadwick tweeted to President Donald Trump, "my friends and teachers were shot. Multiple of my fellow classmates are dead. Do something instead of sending prayers. Prayers won't fix this. But Gun control will prevent it from happening again."[5] Chadwick and other students launched the #NeverAgain Twitter feed "For survivors of the MSD Shooting, by survivors of the MSD." In less than a month, the feed had more than 149,000 followers.

> "Do something instead of sending prayers. Prayers won't fix this. But Gun control will prevent it from happening again."[5]
>
> —Sarah Chadwick, student at MSD

The students did more than take to the airwaves and social media. They also took to the streets. On March 7, 2018, students staged a sit-in at the office of Senate majority leader Mitch McConnell in Washington, DC, demanding that federal lawmakers pass gun control measures. Eight students were arrested for refusing to leave. Students also organized a nationwide school walkout. "On March 24, this movement will take to the streets to demand we end the epidemic of mass shootings,"[6] declared March for Our Lives, a student organization. Three days after the shooting, students held a rally at the Broward County Federal Courthouse in Fort Lauderdale, Florida. MSD senior Emma Gonzalez expressed the frustration of her generation:

The people in the government who are voted into power are lying to us. And us kids seem to be the only ones who notice and are prepared to call BS. They say that tougher gun laws do not decrease gun violence—we call BS! They say a good guy with a gun stops a bad guy with a gun—we call BS! They say guns are just tools like knives and are as dangerous as cars—we call BS! They say that no laws could have been able to prevent the hundreds of senseless tragedies that have occurred—we call BS! That us kids don't know what we're talking about, that we're too young to understand how the government works—we call BS![7]

First Steps

The message seemed to be getting through—at least partially. Less than a month after the shooting, the Florida legislature passed and Governor Rick Scott signed into law the Marjory Stoneman Douglas High School Public Safety Act, a measure raising the age for purchasing rifles from eighteen to twenty-one (people already had

On March 24, 2018, students from Marjory Stoneman Douglas High School in Parkland, Florida—the scene of a February school shooting that killed seventeen people—led the March for Our Lives in Washington, DC, to protest gun violence. Eight hundred thousand people attended the march.

to be twenty-one to purchase handguns). "The hardest thing I've ever had to do as governor is try to find the words to console a parent who has lost their child," Scott said at the signing ceremony. "There are just no words."[8] The new law also created a three-day waiting period on all gun sales, and it banned bump stocks, devices that enable semiautomatic rifles to fire hundreds of rounds a minute. Under a section of the new law known as the Coach Aaron Feis Guardian Program, some teachers will be allowed to carry a firearm at school if both the local school district and local sheriff's department agree. A separate law to ban semiautomatic weapons altogether failed to pass, however.

The MSD protests have rekindled the debate over the place of guns in American society. Mass shootings are only a small part of a much larger pattern of gun violence across the country. The United States leads the world in the total number of gun-related deaths, including homicides, police shootings, and suicides. For decades, politicians have debated about what can be done to reduce the number of gun deaths. Some laws, such as a federal law requiring licensed gun sellers to run background checks on potential gun buyers, have been enacted. Another, banning semiautomatic assault-style weapons, became law in 1994 but expired ten years later. Gun owners have pushed back against further regulation, and more than a dozen states have enacted laws allowing gun owners to carry concealed weapons without any kind of permit. Nevertheless, amid ongoing protests over gun violence—mainly led by students—politicians are vowing that things will be different this time. "Congress cannot and will not just move on from this tragedy," tweeted Representative Ted Deutch, who represents the Florida district that includes Parkland. "The nation will not forget #Parkland. Because this time, we join the #MSDStrong students in declaring, #NeverAgain."[9]

But it has happened again. On May 18, 2018, a seventeen-year-old student opened fire on his high school campus. Authorities say he killed ten people and wounded thirteen others. Many of the dead and injured were fellow students at Santa Fe High School in Southeast Texas.

Chapter One

A Uniquely American Problem

Americans make up less than 5 percent of the world's population yet own between 35 percent and 50 percent of the world's privately held firearms, according to the 2007 Small Arms Survey, the latest global estimate of firearm ownership. Since the survey was taken, the number of firearms in the United States has grown from 277 million to more than 310 million.

A 2017 survey by the Pew Research Center found that 30 percent of Americans own a firearm and 42 percent live in a household with a gun. No other developed nation has as high a percentage of gun owners. The nearest is Switzerland, in which 28.6 percent of the population report having a firearm in the household. Other countries with high levels of ownership include Croatia (14.4 percent), Slovenia (12.9 percent), Macedonia (12.3 percent), Bulgaria (11.4 percent), and Albania (5.7 percent). Gun ownership is lower in northern Europe. Germany has 1.4 million gun owners, or about 1.7 percent of the population. England and Wales have 716,371 gun owners, just 1.2 percent of the population. In North America, Canada has 2 million registered gun owners, or about 5.7 percent of the population—less than a fifth of the American percentage.

A Cultural Legacy

The American affinity for firearms can be traced to the nation's founding. The colonies that formed the United States were the first European holdings to earn their independence through armed revolution. As a result, the founders of the United States held their guns in high regard, viewing them as essential to the cause of freedom and a bulwark against future despots. "What country can preserve its liberties if their rulers are not warned from time to time that their people preserve the spirit of resistance? Let them take arms,"[10] wrote Thomas Jefferson in a 1787 letter to William Stephens Smith, a diplomat who had served as a lieutenant colonel in the Revolutionary War. "To preserve liberty, it is essential that the whole body of people always possess arms, and be taught alike, especially when young, how to use them,"[11] wrote Virginia statesman Richard Henry Lee in 1788. "A free people ought not only to be armed, but disciplined,"[12] stated George Washington in his first address to both houses of Congress on January 8, 1790.

> "To preserve liberty, it is essential that the whole body of people always possess arms, and be taught alike, especially when young, how to use them."[11]
>
> —Richard Henry Lee, Virginia delegate to the Constitutional Congress

Believing that an armed citizenry was essential to the cause of liberty, the nation's founders enshrined the right to bear arms in the US Constitution. "A well regulated militia being necessary to the security of a free State, the right of the People to keep and bear arms shall not be infringed," states the Second Amendment. Only eight other countries have included the right to bear arms in their constitutions, and five of those countries have repealed the guarantee. Today only Guatemala, Mexico, and the United States have constitutions that guarantee their citizens the right to own guns.

At the time of the American Revolution, more than half of the colonists owned guns, according to research by James Lindgren, a law professor at Northwestern University, and Justin L. Heather, an attorney. Reviewing court records of the estates the colonists left behind when they died, known as probate records, Lindgren and Heather found that 54 percent of men and 19 percent of women owned guns in 1774. Forty percent of the people in the Mid-Atlantic colonies owned guns, compared to 50 percent in New England and 69 percent in the South. Gun ownership was

At the time of the American Revolution, more than half of the colonists owned guns. Believing that an armed citizenry was essential to the cause of liberty, the nation's founders enshrined the right to bear arms in the US Constitution.

higher in the South in part because guns were used to deter and suppress slave uprisings. "The odds that large slaveholders would own guns is 4.3 times as high as the odds of gun ownership for estates without large numbers of slaves," write Lindgren and Heather. More people owned guns than cash, books, chairs, and swords or other blade weapons. "The relative odds of a male wealthholder owning a gun were seven times as high as the odds of him owning an edged weapon," write the researchers. They add that the ownership of guns was probably even higher than they estimate. Lindgren and Heather write, "Given that these counts are based on incomplete probate inventories . . . these gun counts are likely to be substantial underestimates."[13]

Gun ownership remained high throughout American history. Guns played a decisive role in the wars against Native Americans as the country expanded westward. Sharpshooters such as Davy Crockett and Annie Oakley were idolized for their shooting skills. The exploits of Old West gunfighters such as Billy the Kid, Bat Mas-

A Student Calls for Political Action

An MSD student, David Hogg, addressed the March for Our Lives rally in Washington, DC. In this excerpt, he calls on young adults to take political action against gun violence.

The cold grasp of corruption shackles the District of Columbia. The winter is over. Change is here. The sun shines on a new day, and the day is ours. First-time voters show up 18 percent of the time at midterm elections. Not anymore. Now, who here is gonna vote in the 2018 election? If you listen real close, you can hear the people in power shaking. They've gotten used to being protective of their position, the safety of inaction. Inaction is no longer safe. And to that, we say: No more. . . .

Ninety-six people die every day from guns in our country, yet most representatives have no public stance on guns. And to that, we say: No more. We are going to make this the voting issue. . . . We are going to make sure the best people get in our elections to run, not as politicians, but as Americans. Because this—this is not cutting it. . . .

Without the persistence—heat—without the persistence of voters and Americans everywhere, getting out to every election, democracy will not flourish. But it can, and it will. So, I say to those politicians that say change will not come, I say: We will not stop until every man, every woman, every child, and every American can live without fear of gun violence. And to that, I say: No more.

Quoted in James Loke Hale, "The Transcript of David Hogg's March for Our Lives Speech Will Bring Tears to Your Eyes," *Bustle*, March 25, 2018. www.bustle.com.

terson, Doc Holliday, and Wyatt Earp were enshrined in legend. Gun-wielding soldiers in the Revolutionary War, Civil War, World War I and II, and even the Global War on Terrorism deepened the allure of firearms. Even the use of guns by gangsters such as Al Capone, Machine Gun Kelly, and Bonnie Parker and Clyde Barrow (Bonnie and Clyde) became part of American lore. Guns figure prominently in countless books, movies, television, programs, and even video games. "America is the gun," summarized *New York Times* columnist Charles M. Blow after the Parkland shooting. "Its very beginning is rooted in gun violence. It is by the barrel that this land was acquired. It is by the barrel that the slave was subdued and his rebellions squashed. And that is to say nothing of our wars."[14]

> "It is by the barrel that this land was acquired. It is by the barrel that the slave was subdued and his rebellions squashed. And that is to say nothing of our wars."[14]
>
> —Charles M. Blow, columnist for the *New York Times*

Comparing Mass Shootings by Country

The proliferation of guns has contributed to the fact that the United States has more mass shootings than any other single country. A 2016 study by the University of Alabama found that the United States had ninety mass shootings between 1966 and 2012. That number was five times greater than that of the Philippines, which had eighteen mass shootings, the second-highest number. The other countries with high numbers of mass shootings during that period are Russia, with fifteen; Yemen, with eleven; and France, with ten. Of course, the population of the United States (324 million people) is roughly the same as these other countries combined (342 million people). And the total number of mass shootings in those countries is fifty-four, compared to the ninety in the United States.

When comparing countries, it is best to compare nations that are similar culturally and economically. For example, Yemen does not compare well with the United States, because it lacks a stable government. The Philippines does not match up well, because it is a poor country with a great deal of violence related to drug cartels. A better comparison for gun violence is with the European Union, a political union made up of twenty-eight developed countries with a combined population of 510 million people. About two-thirds of Americans are immigrants or the descendants of immigrants from countries that belong to the European Union.

As a result, the United States shares many of Europe's political and cultural traditions. A study by the Crime Prevention Research Center, an organization specializing in gun policy, found that from 2009 through 2015, the United States had twenty-five mass shootings and the European Union had nineteen. However, the European Union had more deaths from its mass shootings—230 compared to 199 in the United States. The mass shooting death rate per million people in the European Union was 0.114, which is slightly higher than the US rate of 0.089. In other words, the chances of a person dying in a mass shooting were about the same in the United States and the European Union during that period.

A Global Outlier

Mass shootings make up a small part of all gun violence, which includes homicides, police shootings, and home defense shootings. The United States has a much higher death rate from overall gun violence than do other advanced nations. According to the University of Washington's Institute for Health Metrics and Evaluation (IHME), the United States had 3.85 deaths due to gun violence per 100,000 people in 2016. The US rate was eight times higher than the rate in Canada, thirty-two times higher than the rate in Germany, and fifty-five times higher than the rate in the United Kingdom. "It is a little surprising that a country like ours should have this level of gun violence," says Ali Mokdad, a professor of global health and epidemiology at the IHME. "If you compare us to other well-off countries, we really stand out."[15]

> "It is a little surprising that a country like ours should have this level of gun violence. If you compare us to other well-off countries, we really stand out."[15]
>
> —Ali Mokdad, professor of global health and epidemiology at the IHME

This is not to say that the United States has the world's highest rate of deaths by gun violence. Thirty other countries have higher death rates from gun violence than the United States does,

A soldier patrols a neighborhood in Rio de Janeiro, Brazil, in August 2017 as part of a governmental effort to curb gun violence. Brazil is one of only thirty countries that has a higher death rate from gun violence than the United States.

including Brazil, the Philippines, South Africa, and Thailand. El Salvador, which is rife with gang violence and drug wars, has the world's highest gun violence death rate, with 40.29 deaths per 100,000—more than ten times the rate in the United States. Nevertheless, the United States has a higher rate of gun violence than 164 other countries, including all of the economically advanced nations. In 2015 America's gun homicide rate was twenty-five times greater than the average of other high-income countries.

Sharp Increases

After fifteen years of relative stability, the number of gun-related homicides increased sharply in 2015 and 2016, the latest years

Repeal the Second Amendment

Retired Supreme Court justice John Paul Stevens dissented in the 2008 *District of Columbia v. Heller* decision that broadened the protections of the Second Amendment. In this excerpt from an editorial Stevens wrote following the March 24, 2018, nationwide March for Our Lives demonstrations, he calls for the repeal of the Second Amendment.

Rarely in my lifetime have I seen the type of civic engagement schoolchildren and their supporters demonstrated in Washington and other major cities throughout the country this past Saturday. These demonstrations demand our respect. They reveal the broad public support for legislation to minimize the risk of mass killings of schoolchildren and others in our society.

That support is a clear sign to lawmakers to enact legislation prohibiting civilian ownership of semiautomatic weapons, increasing the minimum age to buy a gun from 18 to 21 years old, and establishing more comprehensive background checks on all purchasers of firearms. But the demonstrators should seek more effective and more lasting reform. They should demand a repeal of the Second Amendment. . . .

That simple but dramatic action would move Saturday's marchers closer to their objective than any other possible reform. It would eliminate the only legal rule that protects sellers of firearms in the United States—unlike every other market in the world. It would make our schoolchildren safer than they have been since [the *Heller* decision in] 2008 and honor the memories of the many, indeed far too many, victims of recent gun violence.

John Paul Stevens, "John Paul Stevens: Repeal the Second Amendment," *New York Times*, March 27, 2018. www.nytimes.com.

for which the Centers for Disease Control and Prevention (CDC), an agency of the federal government, has released its annual death statistics. The CDC reported that there were 12,979 firearm homicides in 2015, up from 10,945 in 2014—a 16 percent jump in just one year. The number rose again in 2016 to 14,415—a 10 percent increase from 2015. Even with the increase, however, the 2016 numbers were 22 percent lower than they were at the nation's peak in 1993, when there were 18,253 firearm homicides in the country. In fact, the gun homicide rate in 2014 was the lowest it had been in the previous thirty-four years.

While the number of gun homicides was dropping by 40 percent from 1993 to 2014, the number of privately owned firearms in the United States was rising by 56 percent, and the number of homes with guns was staying about the same. According to Lane Kenworthy, professor of sociology at the University of California–San Diego:

> The over-time pattern in the US since 1960 suggests little or no effect of guns on the homicide rate. . . . The share of homes that have a gun has been relatively flat throughout the past half century, while the number of guns per person in the country has increased significantly. Neither trend looks to be useful in predicting the homicide rate, which jumped sharply in the 1960s and 1970s and then fell just as sharply beginning in the early–mid 1990s.[16]

While the explosive growth in the number of guns in the United States does not appear to have affected the overall gun homicide rate, it may have contributed to a greater use of guns to commit murder. According to data from the FBI, in 1961—the earliest year for which the FBI has data—about half of all murders were committed with a gun. Thirty years later, in 1990, that figure had grown to 65 percent of all murders. Between 1990 and 2015 the percentage of murders committed with a gun remained between 63 percent and 70 percent. However, in 2015 the share of gun murders rose above 70 percent for the first time. In 2016 guns were used in 73 percent of all murders—the highest rate on record.

Adding Up All Gunshot Deaths

The IHME, CDC, and FBI studies focused on the criminal use of guns. However, gun homicides make up only a portion of the gun-related deaths—roughly a third. About 60 percent of all gun deaths are suicides. The CDC reports that there were 22,938 gun suicides in 2016. When deaths from homicides, suicides, accidents, and all other gun-related causes are added together, the United States had 38,658 gunshot deaths in 2016. Most disturbingly, firearm injuries are the third-leading cause of death among US children aged seventeen and younger, according to a 2017 study published in the medical journal *Pediatrics*.

The United States has far more gunshot deaths than any country in the developed world. According to the CDC, the United States had 11.96 gunshot deaths per 100,000 people in 2016. Numbers are not available from all countries for the same years, but figures from 2014 show Switzerland with the second-highest rate, at 3.01 gunshot deaths per 100,000 people—about one-fourth the US rate. Austria was next at 2.9 deaths per 100,000 people in 2014. France had 2.6 deaths per 100,000 people in 2013, Croatia had 2.35 in 2013, and Canada had 2.05 in 2011—about one-sixth the US rate. All other advanced countries were below 2 gunshot deaths per 100,000 people. The rate in Germany—Europe's most populous country—was 1.01 in 2014, nearly one-twelfth the US rate. The United Kingdom, which founded what later became the United States and shares a similar culture, had a gunshot death rate of 0.22 in 2013—fifty-four times lower than the US rate.

Using the overall gunshot death rate in public policy debates about mass shootings and gun-related crime is deceptive, some gun rights advocates maintain, because suicides and accidents should not be factored into that debate. At the end of 2017, Grant Stinchfield, host of an online news program sponsored by the National Rifle Association (NRA), said, "The final fake news of the year comes in the form of a statistic, the overused 30,000 gun deaths

Two-Year Rise in Gun Deaths—and Still Rising

Data published by the CDC in December 2017 show the number of gun deaths (including suicides) in the United States has increased for two consecutive years. Gun death totals increased in 2015 and again in 2016. The CDC publishes these statistics in its annual year-end summary. Gun Violence Archive (GVA), a nonprofit organization that tracks media and law enforcement reports of shootings, also collects gun death statistics. Its 2017-released count (which excludes most suicides) shows a 3 percent increase in the number of people killed by guns in the United States—an early indicator of a continued rise in gun deaths.

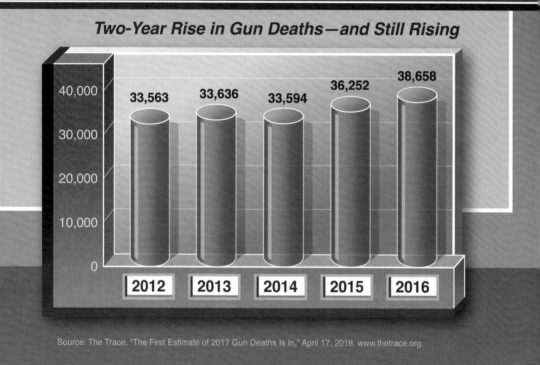

Source: The Trace, "The First Estimate of 2017 Gun Deaths Is In," April 17, 2018. www.thetrace.org.

a year. The left never mentions that two-thirds of those include suicides. Yet it is a number thrown around like confetti. And it's deceptive to say the least."[17] Cydney Hargis, a guns and public safety researcher at Media Matters for America, a media watchdog group, disagrees with Stinchfield. "Stinchfield's claim that 'gun suicides' don't count in gun death totals ignores a vast body of research proving that firearm availability has a direct impact on successful suicide attempts,"[18] writes Hargis in the Media Matters blog.

A Lack of Scientific Data

Hargis might be overstating the case when she calls the research vast, however. In what *Science News* calls the largest comprehensive analysis of research on US gun policy in years, a team led by Andrew R. Morral, a behavioral scientist at the Rand Corporation, a nonpartisan research institute, reviewed thousands of studies on gun policy. But Morral and his team found only sixty-three that used rigorous methods and established cause and effect, and only a few of those focused on gun suicide. "The research literature on gun policies is really very thin,"[19] says Morral. In the area of gun suicide, the team found that in five out of nine gun policy areas, including licensing, waiting periods, and bans on assault weapons, research either had not been conducted or was inconclusive.

David Studdert, a professor of law and of medicine at Stanford University who views gunshot deaths as a public health issue, believes that all gunshot deaths cannot be lumped together when discussing policy. "Gun violence is not one epidemic, but several sub-epidemics, each with very different properties and racial profiles," says Studdert. "While firearm homicide rates are highest among young black men, rates of firearm suicide are highest among middle-aged and elderly white men. These different sub-epidemics clearly call for different policy responses."[20]

> "Gun violence is not one epidemic, but several sub-epidemics, each with very different properties and racial profiles. . . . These different sub-epidemics clearly call for different policy responses."[20]
>
> —David Studdert, professor of law and of medicine at Stanford University

In his study, Morral identified thirteen public policies aimed at reducing the number of gun deaths. Some have been enacted in the United States, but others have not. A few have widespread support, but most are controversial. Unfortunately, Morral found that there is little scientific evidence showing which of these measures have been or would be effective. "There is a need for a factual basis on which to make policy," Morral and his team write. However, the researchers caution against making public policy decisions based on scientific findings only. As they explain:

> This does not mean basing decisions just on facts about which policies will reduce homicides or suicides the most; it means basing decisions on an accurate understanding of the trade-offs that policies entail. . . . These scientific questions about what is true and knowable do not supersede questions of individual rights or Second Amendment rights. Both should be central considerations in policy-making.[21]

Because of its history, its Constitution, and the high percentage of its population that have owned guns since its founding, the United States has less gun regulation than any other advanced country. Many Americans—especially young Americans—look at their country's gun death rate and believe something must be done. "Shootings are happening more and more often," tweeted MSD senior Carly Novell three weeks after the Parkland shooting. "This isn't rare. We need to go to the root of the problem, which is guns."[22]

Chapter Two

A Patchwork of Laws

The United States has many different laws that regulate guns and gun ownership. Some of these laws have been enacted on the national level and affect all Americans, but most have been enacted at the state and local levels. This has left a patchwork of gun laws across the country.

Federalism

The lack of uniformity in gun laws is by design. Having lived under a government with a great deal of power concentrated in the hands of one person—the king of England—the founders of the United States designed a government that spread the power around to the states that make up the union. The Constitution creates a national government to handle things individual states cannot, such as the coining of money, the raising of an army and navy, and the declaration of war on foreign countries. These are known as the Constitution's enumerated powers. Laws and regulations not included in this list are left to the states. "The powers not delegated to the United States by the Constitution, nor prohibited by it to the States, are reserved to the States respectively, or to the people," states the Tenth Amendment. This system is known as federalism.

Gun regulation is one area in which the various states have enacted their own laws. As a matter of fact, no two states have identical gun laws. Some of the differences are small, but others are large. For example, thirteen states, including Arizona, Missouri, and Maine, allow gun owners to carry a weapon concealed in a purse or holster without any kind of permit. On the other hand, eight states, including the two most populous—California and New York—have "may issue" laws that allow concealed carry with a permit given only if the person meets strict standards. One of these states—Hawaii—did not issue any concealed carry permits in 2016. Since the state's concealed carry permit is valid for only one year, Hawaii effectively banned the practice. The remaining twenty-nine states have "must issue" laws that allow concealed carry with a permit that the state is required to issue as long as the applicant is qualified. The qualifications vary from state to state. This is different from the gun policies of most countries, which tend to have one national law regulating firearms.

> "The powers not delegated to the United States by the Constitution, nor prohibited by it to the States, are reserved to the States respectively, or to the people."
>
> —Tenth Amendment to the US Constitution

Benefits of Federalism

By allowing the states to set and test their own policies, the federal system creates what have been called "laboratories of democracy." This phrase originated with Supreme Court justice Louis Brandeis, who wrote, "It is one of the happy incidents of the federal system that a single courageous State may, if its citizens choose, serve as a laboratory; and try novel social and economic experiments without risk to the rest of the country."[23] This system allows for gradual change as policies prove effective before being adopted by the entire nation. It keeps the country from careening from one untested policy to another.

Federalism also gives the states the ability to change their policies quickly, rather than waiting for the entire nation to reach a consensus. For example, in 2004 a national ban on semiautomatic guns, sometimes known as assault weapons, was set to expire. Four states—Hawaii,

> "It is one of the happy incidents of the federal system that a single courageous State may, if its citizens choose, serve as a laboratory; and try novel social and economic experiments without risk to the rest of the country."[23]
>
> —Justice Louis Brandeis of the US Supreme Court

US Supreme Court justice Louis Brandeis (pictured) described federalism as enabling states to act as laboratories to test the effectiveness of government policies before they are adopted by the nation at large. This system has resulted in a patchwork of gun laws across the country.

Maryland, Massachusetts, and New York—quickly passed their own assault weapons bans before the federal law expired. Similarly, in 2009 only two states—Alaska and Vermont—allowed concealed carry of guns without a permit. By 2017 the number had expanded to thirteen. During this time, Congress enacted no nationwide changes to gun laws.

The patchwork of laws created under federalism creates gaps. For example, a person who meets the standards for owning a gun in one state might not meet them in another, but there is almost nothing to stop that person from carrying a gun into a state with stricter gun laws. The patchwork of laws creates other problems, as well. For example, a person carrying a concealed weapon who drives through several states could move in and out of different legal jurisdictions, and in and out of violating the law, sometimes without even knowing it.

Two Views of State Laws

In an annual survey, the gun-enthusiast magazine *Guns & Ammo* rates the gun laws in all fifty states in four areas: the right to carry weapons both visible and concealed, access to assault rifles, legal protection for people who use deadly force for self-defense, and the ability to obtain certain weapons covered by the National Firearms Act (NFA). First passed in 1934, the NFA regulates the sale, transfer, and possession of machine guns, suppressors (silencers), short-barreled rifles, short-barreled shotguns, and other weapons. States have the right to further restrict these items and even ban them outright, which some states have done. The Giffords Law Center to Prevent Gun Violence, an organization that advocates for stricter gun control, also rates each state's gun laws. In addition to concealed carry and assault weapons laws, the Giffords Law Center grades states on background checks, child access prevention, domestic violence restrictions, and extreme-risk protection orders. Together, the rankings that the *Guns & Ammo* and Giffords Law Center lists give to the fifty states illustrate the patchwork of gun laws in the United States.

Not surprisingly, the two lists are near opposites. The state that *Guns & Ammo* ranks as the best for gun owners—Arizona— ranks forty-seventh on the Giffords Law Center list for gun safety. Arizona allows people to carry both visible and concealed guns without a permit, has no further restrictions on the purchase of NFA-regulated weapons or assault rifles, and has strong "stand your ground" laws that allow gun owners to use their weapons for self-defense without having to first retreat. By contrast, the state that the Giffords Law Center ranks first for the strength of its gun laws—California—ranks forty-sixth on the *Guns & Ammo* list.

California allows concealed carry only with strict "may issue" permits; bans most assault rifles; prohibits the sale, transfer, manufacture, and possession of large-capacity ammunition magazines; requires all gun sales to be processed through a licensed dealer who runs a background check; and prevents gun ownership by domestic abusers and people with mental health problems.

The two lists are not always total opposites, however. Because the Giffords Law Center gives special weight to laws regulating who can own a gun, it ranks Utah twenty-seventh, even though it is ranked as the sixth-best state for gun owners by *Guns & Ammo*. The Giffords Law Center gives Utah credit for having a strong law that prevents domestic abusers from buying guns, requires them to turn over any guns they own to law enforcement officials, and requires them to provide proof to a court that they have done so. On the other hand, Utah has a "must issue" permit system for concealed weapons and has no further restrictions on the purchase of NFA-regulated weapons or assault weapons. Overall, the Giffords Law Center gives Utah a failing grade for the strength of its gun laws. Utah is not alone. The Giffords Law Center gives twenty-five of the fifty states a grade of F for their gun laws. Only six states receive an A.

Cities can also pass their own gun laws. For example, Chicago, Illinois, and some of its suburbs passed laws banning assault rifles and large ammunition magazines. Despite such bans, Chicago had more homicides than any American city in 2017 (650). It ranked fifth out of American's fifty largest cities for homicide rate, with 24 homicides per 100,000 people. Notably, despite its strict gun control laws, Chicago had a homicide rate more than six times higher than some large cities with minimal gun restrictions, including Mesa, Arizona (3.7); Austin, Texas (3.1); and El Paso, Texas (2.8).

It might seem logical to conclude that Chicago's gun laws are ineffective, but this is not necessarily the case. Chicago is a victim of the patchwork of American gun laws. Two of the states that border Illinois—Wisconsin and Indiana—have permissive gun

An NRA Member Backs a Ban on Assault Weapons

Brian Mast, a Republican, is the representative for Florida's Eighteenth Congressional District, a US Army veteran who served in the war in Afghanistan, and a longtime member of the NRA. In this excerpt, he discusses why he supports a ban on assault weapons.

I conceal and carry a 9-millimeter pistol most days because I know the threats, and I don't want to die because I am unprepared to return fire. I also know that I am made less safe by the threat of tactical rifles. I am confident I can eliminate an active shooter who is attacking with a pistol because the attacker would have to be close to me. But the defense my concealed 9-millimeter affords me is largely gone if the attacker is firing from beyond 40 yards, as he could easily do with the AR-15. . . .

The Second Amendment is unimpeachable. It guarantees the right of citizens to defend themselves. I accept, however, that it does not guarantee that every civilian can bear any and all arms. . . .

Therefore, I support the following:

Defining what constitutes an assault or tactical firearm and not allowing them for future purchase—just as we already prohibit the purchase of fully automatic firearms. The exact definition of assault weapon will need to be determined. But we should all be able to agree that the civilian version of the very deadly weapon that the Army issued to me should certainly qualify.

Brian Mast, "I'm Republican. I Appreciate Assault Weapons. And I Support a Ban," *New York Times*, February 23, 2018. www.nytimes.com.

laws. Not surprisingly, many guns used in crimes in Chicago are purchased in these neighboring states. According to the Bureau of Alcohol, Tobacco, Firearms and Explosives (ATF), more than half of the firearms recovered from criminals in Illinois came from out of state. Similarly, a 2015 study found that more than 60 percent of new guns used in Chicago gang-related crimes between 2009 and 2013 were bought in other states. One-third of the out-of-state guns were purchased in Indiana—less than an hour's drive from Chicago.

An Individual Right

At one point, Chicago, Washington, DC, and other cities passed laws that banned all handguns inside the city limits. This gave rise to a legal case that the US Supreme Court called the "first in-depth examination of the Second Amendment,"[24] *District of Columbia v. Heller* (2008). The case was brought by Dick Heller, a Washington, DC, special police officer who was authorized to carry a handgun while on duty at the Federal Judicial Center. He applied for a registration certificate for a handgun that he wished to keep at home. The city refused, as per its policy. "The District of Columbia generally prohibits the possession of handguns," summarized the Supreme Court. "It is a crime to carry an unregistered firearm, and the registration of handguns is prohibited."[25] In addition, the city also required residents to keep lawfully owned firearms, such as rifles, unloaded, disassembled, or bound by a trigger lock in the home. Heller filed a lawsuit on Second Amendment grounds seeking to bar the city from enforcing its ban on the registration of handguns and the requirement that guns have a trigger lock, which prevents the owner from having a working gun in the home in case of an emergency, such as self-defense.

A district court dismissed Heller's lawsuit, but the Court of Appeals for the District of Columbia Circuit reversed that finding. It held that the Second Amendment protects an individual's right to possess firearms. It also found that the city's total ban on handguns, as well as its requirement that firearms in the home be kept nonfunctional, violated the right to keep and bear arms.

In a 5–4 decision, the Supreme Court affirmed the Court of Appeals ruling. As Justice Antonin Scalia wrote for the majority:

We hold that the District's ban on handgun possession in the home violates the Second Amendment, as does its prohibition against rendering any lawful firearm in the home operable for the purpose of immediate self-defense. . . . The inherent right of self-defense has been central to the Second Amendment right. The handgun ban amounts to a prohibition of an entire class of "arms" that is overwhelmingly chosen by American society for that lawful purpose. The prohibition extends, moreover, to the home, where the need for defense of self, family, and property is most acute. Under any of the standards of scrutiny that we have applied to enumerated constitutional rights, banning from the home "the most preferred firearm in the nation to 'keep' and use for protection of one's home and family," would fail constitutional muster.[26]

The high court went out of its way to point out that other restrictions on gun ownership are constitutional. "Nothing in our opinion should be taken to cast doubt on long-standing prohibitions on the possession of firearms by felons and the mentally ill, or laws forbidding the carrying of firearms in sensitive places such as schools and government buildings, or laws imposing conditions and qualifications on the commercial sale of arms,"[27] wrote Scalia. What is not constitutional, the court said, is an outright ban on the private ownership of firearms for lawful purposes like self-defense.

> "The inherent right of self-defense has been central to the Second Amendment right."[26]
>
> —Supreme Court justice Antonin Scalia

National Gun Laws

One way to repair the patchwork of gun laws would be to pass seamless nationwide gun laws. This has been done several times in the nation's history. The first federal gun law was the NFA in 1934. Congress adopted this law following an investigation into gangland violence in the 1920s and 1930s. Congress and the public were particularly concerned about the use of the Thompson submachine gun, or tommy gun, by gangsters in the St. Valentine's Day Massacre and other gangland slayings. The law placed a $200 tax (equivalent to $3,500 today) on the manufacture or sale of guns and sawed-off shotguns. This made the guns too expensive for ordinary people to buy. Criminals who purchased such guns without paying the tax were subject to a fine equal to $35,000 today. In addition, the law required all sales of the regulated guns to be recorded in a national registry.

Two gangsters, Jack Miller and Frank Layton, challenged the constitutionality of the NFA on Second Amendment grounds. Miller and Layton had been charged with taking a 12-gauge shotgun with a barrel less than 18 inches (45.7 cm) long across state lines without having registered the weapon. In *United States v. Miller*, the Supreme Court found that such a weapon was not protected by the Second Amendment because it had no "reasonable relation to the preservation or efficiency of a well regulated militia."[28] In this case, the court did not delve into the question of whether the Second Amendment guaranteed an individual right to own a gun for self-protection. That was left to the court to examine in the *Heller* case seventy-five years later. "*Miller* stands only for the proposition that the Second Amendment right, whatever its nature, extends only to certain types of weapons,"[29] the court stated in *Heller*.

Another federal gun law set restrictions on who could purchase guns. Congress passed the Brady Handgun Violence Prevention Act on November 11, 1993, and President Bill Clinton signed it into law nineteen days later. Also known as the Brady Act, it was named after James Brady, the press secretary to President Ronald Reagan, who was seriously wounded in an assassination attempt on the president in 1981. Brady's injury left him partially paralyzed for life. The investigation into the assassination found that the shooter, John Hinckley Jr., had been under psychiatric care before buying the gun he used in the shooting. He also gave false information on the gun purchase application—an

President Bill Clinton signs into law the Brady Handgun Violence Prevention Act in November 1993 as former White House press secretary James Brady, for whom the bill was named, looks on. The law tightened restrictions on who could purchase handguns.

act that was a felony offense. However, there was no way for the pawn shop that sold the gun to know the information was false.

The Brady Act was created in part to stop people like Hinckley from having access to firearms. It makes it a crime for a person to buy a gun under certain conditions, including if the person has been convicted of a crime punishable by imprisonment for a term exceeding one year; is a fugitive from justice; has been committed to a mental institution or found by a court to have mental defects; is subject to a court order that restrains the person from harassing, stalking, or threatening an intimate partner or child of such intimate partner; or has been convicted of domestic violence. To help the gun dealer know whether a potential buyer is

A Partisan Divide

Ruth Igielnik and Anna Brown are research analysts for the Pew Research Center. In this excerpt, they describe key takeaways from a 2017 survey that shows a partisan divide among Americans on gun ownership issues.

For most gun owners, owning a firearm is tied to their sense of personal freedom. While gun owners and non-owners tend to agree on most top-tier constitutional rights, one key difference is the extent to which owners associate the right to own guns with their own personal sense of freedom. Roughly three-quarters of gun owners (74%) say this right is essential, compared with 35% of non-gun owners.

Partisanship is strongly correlated with views about the importance of gun ownership as a guaranteed right. Among gun owners, Republicans and Republican-leaning independents are about twice as likely as Democrats and Democratic leaners to say owning a gun is essential to their freedom (91% vs. 43%). In fact, Republican non-owners are more likely than Democratic owners to view the right to own guns as essential to their freedom (61% vs. 43%). . . .

There is also a partisan divide on views of gun policy, and these differences remain even after controlling for gun ownership. For example, Republican gun owners are much more resistant than Democratic owners to banning assault-style weapons and high-capacity magazines as well as creating a database to track gun sales. And Republicans are much more open than Democrats to proposals that would expand gun rights, such as allowing people to carry concealed guns in more places and allowing teachers and officials to carry guns in K–12 schools.

Ruth Igielnik and Anna Brown, "Key Takeaways on Americans' Views of Guns and Gun Ownership," Pew Research Center, June 22, 2017. www.pewresearch.org.

eligible to purchase a gun, the bill mandated the creation of the National Instant Criminal Background Check System (NICS), an electronic database maintained by the FBI. NICS background checks have become routine and take only minutes to complete.

Since NICS was launched in 1998, more than 230 million checks have been processed, leading to more than 1.3 million denials of sales. Although the Supreme Court did not mention the Brady Act by name in the *Heller* decision, the court was clearly referring to it and similar state laws when it announced that its ruling did not affect laws that restrict gun ownership by felons and the mentally ill.

The Assault Weapons Ban of 1994

The most recent federal gun law Congress passed was the Public Safety and Recreational Firearms Use Protection Act, a subsection of the Violent Crime Control and Law Enforcement Act of 1994. Signed into law by Clinton, the Public Safety and Recreational Firearms Use Protection Act made it unlawful for a person to manufacture, transfer, or possess a semiautomatic assault weapon. A semiautomatic weapon is different from a fully automatic weapon, known as a machine gun. With a machine gun, the user can pull the trigger once and hold it down to discharge multiple rounds of ammunition. A semiautomatic weapon, by contrast, requires a separate pull of the trigger to fire each cartridge. The part of a semiautomatic gun that is automated is the loading of cartridges into the barrel chamber, or breech. A semiautomatic weapon uses a portion of the energy of a firing cartridge to extract the fired cartridge case and load the next round. As a result, the user does not have to reload the weapon after each shot. This differs from a bolt-action rifle, for instance, in which the user must manipulate the handle of a bolt to open the breech and eject or remove the spent cartridge before reloading the gun by hand. The assault weapons ban also prohibited the manufacture of large-capacity ammunition magazines. Because of these provisions, the Public Safety and Recreational Firearms Use Protection Act is often referred to as the assault weapons ban.

Although the language of the bill was sweeping, it was riddled with loopholes. For example, it allowed people who already owned assault weapons to keep them. It also exempted the sale and manufacture of new semiautomatic rifles and shotguns with magazines that held five rounds or fewer. The law included a "sunset" provision that meant it would expire in ten years. Congress did not renew the law in 2004 and has not passed a similar law since. However, seven states—California, Connecticut, Hawaii, Maryland, Massachusetts, New Jersey, and New York—either already had their own assault weapons bans or passed them after the law expired. As with other gun laws, not all the state bans are the same. For example, Hawaii bans semiautomatic pistols but not assault rifles or shotguns. The other states define the guns and magazines differently. The result is a hodgepodge of assault weapons bans.

Several cities have also passed assault weapons bans. In addition to Chicago, Highland Park, and other Illinois cities, Boston, Washington, DC, and East Chicago and Gary, Indiana, restrict the sale and ownership of assault weapons. The law passed in 2013 by the city of Highland Park, a suburb of Chicago, reads, "No person shall manufacture, sell, offer for display for sale, give, lend, transfer ownership of, acquire or possess any Assault Weapon or Large Capacity Magazine."[30] The East Chicago and Gary laws were invalidated by a statewide law passed in 2011.

A semiautomatic weapon like the rifle pictured here reloads a cartridge after each shot, allowing many rounds to be fired in a short period of time. Gun control advocates say such weapons should be banned among ordinary citizens.

Smith & Wesson M&P15
Semi-Automatic Assault Rifle
ake/model used at Aurora, Colorado movie theater shooting
12 people killed, 58 injured

Constitutional Limits on Certain Weapons

In 2013 the Illinois State Rifle Association and Arie Friedman, a Highland Park pediatrician, challenged the Highland Park ban on Second Amendment grounds. The Court of Appeals for the Seventh Circuit upheld the law, stating, "Unlike the District of Columbia's ban on handguns, Highland Park's ordinance leaves residents with many self-defense options."[31] In a 7–2 vote, the Supreme Court decided to let the Seventh Circuit's decision stand. Justice Clarence Thomas dissented, and Justice Antonin Scalia, who wrote the court's decision in *Heller*, joined the dissent. "Roughly five million Americans own AR-style semiautomatic rifles," wrote Thomas. "The overwhelming majority of citizens who own and use such rifles do so for lawful purposes, including self-defense and target shooting. Under our precedents, that is all that is needed for citizens to have a right under the Second Amendment to keep such weapons."[32] The majority of the court disagreed, possibly paving the way for a future national ban on military-style weapons. "The Supreme Court has now signaled that this is consistent with [the] Second Amendment," said Mike McLively, a staff attorney at the Giffords Law Center to Prevent Gun Violence. "This could become a national model."[33] That is exactly what many of the MSD shooting survivors, the March for Our Lives student protesters, and millions of other Americans hope will happen.

> **"Unlike the District of Columbia's ban on handguns, Highland Park's ordinance leaves residents with many self-defense options."[31]**
>
> —Court of Appeals for the Seventh Circuit

Chapter Three

Strengthening Gun Laws

Horrified by the endless stream of mass shootings and outraged by the high level of gun violence in the United States, students and adults are once again calling on Congress to replace the patchwork of gun laws with a seamless national standard. Politicians have also entered the fray. Senator Charles Schumer of New York, who wrote an early draft of the bill that became the Brady Act, is calling for stronger background checks. Senator Dianne Feinstein of California, who authored the first Assault Weapons Ban, introduced a new, tougher one. Some of the ideas—such as a mandatory buyback of existing guns—are new. Others, such as banning large semiautomatic gun magazines, are old. Some people are even calling for a repeal of the Second Amendment and the banning of guns altogether. "Americans who claim to be outraged by gun crimes should want to do something more than tinker at the margins of a legal regime that most of the developed world rightly considers nuts," writes *New York Times* columnist Bret Stephens. "They should want to change it fundamentally and permanently. There is only one way to do this: Repeal the Second Amendment."[34]

Gun Control Goals

On the March for Our Lives website, the MSD students state their views on what should be done. "We call on all the adults in Congress elected to represent us, to pass legislation that will protect and save children from gun violence," the students write. They advance three main proposals for new laws to reduce gun violence. First is a ban on the sale of assault weapons. "No civilian should be able to access these weapons of war, which should be restricted for use by our military and law enforcement only," state the students. "These guns have no other purpose than to fire as many bullets as possible and indiscriminately kill anything they are pointed at with terrifying speed." Second is to prohibit the sale of high-capacity magazines. "Limiting the number of bullets a gun can discharge at one time will at least force any shooter to stop and reload, giving children a chance to escape," write the students. Third, the students call for better background checks, specifically, "closing the loophole in our background check law that allows dangerous people who shouldn't be allowed to purchase firearms to slip through the cracks and buy guns online or at gun shows."[35] Some of these proposals resemble laws that are already in place at the state and city levels. Each faces its own challenges to being enacted at the federal level.

> "We call on all the adults in Congress elected to represent us, to pass legislation that will protect and save children from gun violence."[35]
>
> —March for Our Lives, a student organization protesting gun violence

Unlike licensed gun dealers, private sellers at gun shows like the one pictured here are not required to run a background check on those to whom they sell guns. This is known as the "gun show loophole," and gun reform advocates say it should be eliminated.

Banning Automatic Weapons

The March for Our Lives description of semiautomatic rifles suggests that they are machine guns. They are not. The user of an assault rifle cannot hold down the trigger to fire multiple rounds the way a machine gun user can. Machine guns are already illegal, outlawed by the Firearm Owners' Protection Act of 1986.

Assault rifles can be made to fire at a rate similar to that of a machine gun, however, using an accessory known as a bump stock. These devices harness the gun's recoil energy to bump the trigger against shooter's finger, converting semiautomatic firearms into machine guns. Mass shooter Stephen Paddock used bump stocks on semiautomatic rifles to spray more than one thousand rounds of ammunition into the crowd on the Las Vegas Strip in just ten minutes in October 2017.

Following the Parkland shooting, President Donald Trump said he favored a ban on bump stocks. At the president's direction, Attorney General Jeff Sessions reclassified bump stocks so that they fell under the machine gun prohibition of the Firearm Owners' Protection Act. A March 23, 2018, statement from Sessions said:

> Today the Department of Justice is publishing for public comment a proposed rulemaking that would define "machinegun" to include bump stock–type devices under federal law—effectively banning them. After the senseless attack in Las Vegas, this proposed rule is a critical step in our effort to reduce the threat of gun violence that is in keeping with the Constitution and the laws passed by Congress.[36]

A New Assault Weapons Ban

Banning assault weapons themselves is much more complicated. A new ban would have to be passed by both the House of Representatives and the Senate, not be vetoed by the president, and survive legal challenges that would likely be decided by the Su-

The NRA's Financial Support Is Overstated

Jeff Stein is a journalist. In this excerpt, he discusses the influence of NRA financial contributions on national gun policy.

The National Rifle Association donates millions of dollars every year to Republican lawmakers in Congress. And those same Republicans line up uniformly to block proposed gun control legislation.

The implication of these two facts appears obvious: Politicians are refusing to stem the bloodshed of gun violence because they're getting what amounts to a legal bribe from lobbyists. . . .

But when you talk to experts who study the way money influences our political system, they say this account is wrong—or, at least, often badly oversimplified. The NRA may exert a massive and real influence on Washington, DC, but its campaign contributions can't possibly be the corrupting agent singlehandedly thwarting meaningful action on gun control, as many of the analyses above suggest.

According to the Center for Responsive Politics, the NRA gave close to $1 million to Republican senators' PACs [political action committees] in 2014—or about 1 percent of the $67 million they raised that year. . . .

The donations themselves are clearly not the reason Republican lawmakers fear opposing the NRA—the much bigger threat the gun rights group poses is its ability to mobilize and excite huge numbers of voters. . . .

Of course, none of this means that it wouldn't be good to try to root money out of politics. It just means that doing so wouldn't lead to the sweeping gun control so many liberals hope is only being held back by our campaign finance system.

Jeff Stein, "The NRA Is a Powerful Political Force—but Not Because of Its Money," Vox, October 5, 2017. www.vox.com.

preme Court. Following the Parkland shootings, Representative David N. Cicilline of Rhode Island introduced an assault weapons ban in the House. The bill attracted 167 cosponsors. The bill is similar to legislation introduced in the Senate in 2017 by Senator

Feinstein. Feinstein's measure has 26 cosponsors. Both bills use language and definitions from the expired Assault Weapons Ban of 1994, although the list of banned guns has been updated to include dozens of new semiautomatic weapons.

A new assault weapons ban faces many hurdles. For one thing, it is not clear whether the 1994 Assault Weapons Ban had any effect on gun violence or gun deaths. The US Department of Justice funded three studies on the effects of the ban. In the last of the studies, published in 2004, a team from the University of Pennsylvania led by Christopher S. Koper found that there was "no discernible reduction in the lethality and injuriousness of gun violence"[37] during the ten years the ban was in effect. In part, the researchers said, this was because assault weapons were used in only 2 percent of gun crimes before the ban, so any reduction would have been small to begin with. In addition, 1.5 million pre-ban assault weapons were already in the hands of private owners at the time the ban took effect. These weapons could be and were lawfully used throughout the ban. At a summit on reducing gun violence, held at Johns Hopkins University in 2013, Koper said, "In general we found, really, very, very little evidence, almost none, that gun violence was becoming any less lethal or any less injurious during this time frame. So on balance, we concluded that the ban had not had a discernible impact on gun crime during the years it was in effect."[38]

Koper and his team wrote that the 1994 ban might have had a greater effect if it had been extended, because the exempted guns would have gradually gone out of use. "The ban did not appear to affect gun violence during the time it was in effect," Koper said at the summit. "But there is some evidence to suggest that it may have modestly reduced shootings had it been in effect for a longer period."[39] One problem with enacting a new ban is that there are now five to ten times as many assault weapons in existence as when the 1994 ban went into effect. The assault weapons ban introduced by Cicilline would leave those guns in the hands of their owners, meaning that the effects of a new assault weapons ban would again be gradual at best.

The Australian Buyback

A possible solution to this would be for the government to buy back the existing assault weapons to take them out of circulation. This is what the government of Australia did in 1996 after a twenty-eight-year-old man armed with two assault rifles shot and killed thirty-five people and injured eighteen others in what was known as the Port Arthur massacre. In 1996 the Australian government enacted the National Firearms Agreement. The law banned certain semiautomatic rifles and shotguns and imposed

In response to a mass shooting that killed thirty-five people there in 1996, the government of Australia banned certain guns and instituted a program to buy back the banned weapons from owners. The program collected more than 650,000 guns over four years' time.

stricter licensing and registration requirements for all guns. It also required the people who already owned the banned weapons to turn them in to the government. In exchange, the government paid the owners for the assessed value of the weapons they surrendered. The government funded the mandatory buyback pro-

Would a Gun Ban for Young Adults Be Constitutional?

Raising the age limit for buying and owning a firearm would raise serious constitutional issues, according to authors and attorneys David Kopel and Joseph Greenlee. In this excerpt, they write that preventing an entire group of legal adults from owning a gun is unconstitutional.

Besides violating the laws of some states and cities, firearms bans for young adults also violate the Constitution. In *District of Columbia v. Heller* (2008), the Supreme Court reiterated that "[c]onstitutional rights are enshrined with the scope they were understood to have when the people adopted them." When the Second Amendment was adopted, there were no firearms restrictions on 18-to-20-year-olds, and they were included in every militia across the country. . . .

Males aged 18–20 have a relatively higher violent crime rate than most older age groups. This might be a rationale for special licensing procedures, but not for a ban on the peaceable and law-abiding. Moreover, a ban on 18-to-20-year-old-women makes no sense, since that group is much less violent than the average adult.

Singling out any group for a civil rights ban because of the misbehavior of a tiny minority of the group is collective punishment, and is unjust. All social science data show that males are much more violent than females. That does not justify a gun ban for all males. If statistics show that members of certain races, ethnicities, or religions are relatively more violent, statistically, that does not justify prohibition for the very large non-violent majorities of those groups.

David Kopel and Joseph Greenlee, "Gun Ban for Young Adults Would Be Wholly Unconstitutional," *Hill* (Washington, DC), March 13, 2018. http://thehill.com.

gram by increasing the country's Medicare tax by 12 percent for one year—from 1.5 percent of income to 1.7 percent of income. Over the next four years, the country collected more than 650,000 guns at the cost of 500 million Australian dollars.

Since the buyback, there have been no more mass shootings in Australia. However, in four of the six years following the buyback, the number of murders actually rose from pre-1996 levels. Since 2002 the Australian murder rate has declined to the lowest level in twenty-five years. A 2006 study by researchers at the School of Public Health of the University of Sydney in Australia found the law to be effective. "Australia's 1996 gun law reforms were followed by more than a decade free of fatal mass shootings, and accelerated declines in firearm deaths, particularly suicides," write the researchers. "Total homicide rates followed the same pattern. Removing large numbers of rapid-firing firearms from civilians may be an effective way of reducing mass shootings, firearm homicides and firearm suicides."[40]

However, murder rates also fell during the same period in countries that did not change their gun laws, including the United States. Wang-Sheng Lee of Royal Melbourne Institute of Technology and Sandy Suardi of the University of Wollongong view the same data differently. In 2010 they published a study on the effects of the Australian buyback on gun deaths using different statistical tests on the same data that the University of Sydney researchers had used. "The results of these tests suggest that the [National Firearms Agreement] did not have any large effects on reducing firearm homicide or suicide rates,"[41] write the researchers.

A 2011 study of the Australian ban by David Hemenway and Mary Vriniotis of the Harvard Injury Control Research Center found that the gun murder rate fell from 0.43 per 100,000 people in the seven years before the ban to 0.25 per 100,000 for the seven years after the ban was enacted. The gun suicide rate also fell, from 2.6 per 100,000 in the seven years before the ban to 1.1 per 100,000 in the seven years afterward. However, Hemenway and Vriniotis write that it is difficult to determine whether the law caused the lower gun death rates, since the rates were already falling before the ban was enacted. "No study has explained why gun deaths were falling, or why they might be expected to continue to fall. Yet most studies generally assumed that they would have continued to drop without the [National Firearms Agreement]," they write. Nevertheless, the researchers seem to endorse the ban, saying, "Whether or not one wants to attribute the effects as being due to the law, everyone should be pleased with what happened in Australia after the [National Firearms Agreement]—the elimination of firearm massacres (at least up to the present) and an immediate, and continuing, reduction in firearm suicide and firearm homicide."[42]

An assault weapons ban would face an uphill political battle. Forty-three US states currently allow the sale and possession of assault weapons. At least 5 million Americans own semiautomatic rifles, and tens of millions own semiautomatic pistols. To become law, an assault weapons ban would not only have to pass the House, it would need sixty votes to pass in the Senate. That means that just forty-one senators—less than half the number of senators from states that currently allow the weapons to be owned—could stop the bill from becoming law.

High-Capacity Magazines

The March for Our Lives's second agenda item—banning high-capacity magazines—stands a better chance of becoming law. The bill introduced in the House outlaws large-capacity ammunition feeding devices, which it defines as "a magazine, belt, drum, feed strip, or similar device . . . that has an overall capacity of, or that can be readily restored, changed, or converted to accept, more than 10 rounds of ammunition."[43] Eight states have already outlawed high-capacity magazines. The devices were part of the original assault weapons ban, and some political leaders who oppose banning assault weapons have shown some willingness to consider legislation to ban large-capacity magazines. "I have traditionally not supported looking at magazine clip size and after this and some of the details I have learned about it, I am reconsidering that position," said Senator Marco Rubio of Florida at a town hall meeting held in the wake of the Parkland shooting. "While it may not prevent an attack, it may save lives in an attack. That is something I believe that we can reach a compromise [on] in this country, and that I'm willing to reconsider."[44]

The final item on the March for Our Lives legislative agenda—background checks—has the best chance of being enacted. Federal law already requires any business or person dealing in firearms to be licensed by the ATF. The penalty for dealing in firearms without a license is harsh—up to five years in prison, a fine of up to $250,000, or both. The law applies to anyone engaged in the business of dealing in firearms, regardless of the location in which the firearm sales are conducted. "A person can be engaged in the business of dealing in firearms even if the person only conducts firearm transactions at gun shows or through the internet,"[45] states the ATF website. Anyone purchasing a gun through a federally licensed gun seller must pass an NICS background check administered by the FBI.

> "I have traditionally not supported looking at magazine clip size and after this and some of the details I have learned about it, I am reconsidering that position."[44]
>
> —Marco Rubio, US senator

The Private Sale Loophole

The March for Our Lives website refers to "closing the loophole in our background check law that allows dangerous people . . . to slip through the cracks and buy guns online or at gun shows."[46] This loophole is often called the *gun show loophole*. Under federal law, the only people who can sell guns online or at gun shows without running a background check are private individuals, not licensed gun dealers. Private owners can sell guns online, at flea markets, and in many other ways—including at some gun shows.

The phrase *gun show loophole* is misleading, critics observe, because it suggests that all gun show sales are exempt from background checks. "Criticisms of the 'gun show loophole' imply that federal regulations allow otherwise prohibited retail purchases of firearms at gun shows," writes Nicholas J. Johnson, a professor at Fordham University School of Law. "This implication is false. The real criticism is leveled at secondary market sales by private citizens."[47] University of California–Los Angeles law professor Adam Winkler agrees. "There is a huge loophole in federal law, but it isn't for gun shows," says Winkler. "What is called the gun-show loophole is misnamed. It should be the 'private sale loophole' or the 'background check loophole.'"[48]

> "What is called the gun-show loophole is misnamed. It should be the 'private sale loophole' or the 'background check loophole."[48]
>
> —Adam Winkler, law professor at the University of California–Los Angeles

One way of closing this loophole would be to ban private sellers from participating in gun shows. Another would be to require a private seller's sale to go through a Federal Firearms License (FFL) holder at the show so that the background check is performed. A third would be to have an ATF official at a gun show to process sales by private sellers. However, none of these actions would affect private transfers of firearms in other settings, which make up the vast majority of sales without background checks. According to Johnson, half of all gun sales involve private individuals, not firearms dealers. "With nearly half of gun transfers involving private trades out of the existing inventory, people who complain about the gun show loophole can really only be satisfied by a flat ban on private transfers—e.g., requiring all transfers go through an FFL, who will route the buyer through the NICS,"[49] writes Johnson. A truly universal background check would have to cover all private weapons transfers, including transfers between family members, friends, and work colleagues.

Ten states and the District of Columbia already require background checks for all firearm sales by private individuals. Two more states—Maryland and Pennsylvania—require private sellers of handguns to run background checks. Eight other states require the gun buyers to obtain a gun-purchasing license, which involves passing a background check. Private sellers are required to see this license before they sell a gun to someone. This achieves the same result as having the seller run the background check.

The Charleston Loophole

The NICS has another deficiency, sometimes called the "Charleston loophole." Under current law, the FBI has three business days to determine whether a potential buyer is eligible to purchase a gun. If the background check is inconclusive at the end of the three-day period, the seller is free to sell the gun to the potential buyer. According to the news website ThinkProgress, the FBI did not complete background checks within three business days in 3.59 percent of the 8.6 million gun background checks it conducted in 2017. That means more than 308,000 prospective buyers were eligible to purchase weapons without a background check. This is exactly what happened in the case of Dylann Roof, the mass shooter who killed nine people at a predominantly black church in Charleston, South Carolina, in 2015. Roof should have failed the background check because he previously admitted to possessing illegal drugs. However, the FBI failed to complete the check in the allotted time, and Roof was able to buy a semiautomatic pistol.

If the FBI finds after more than three business days that a person was not eligible to purchase a gun, it can ask the ATF to confiscate the firearm. In 2017 the ATF retrieved 4,170 firearms that dealers had sold to prohibited buyers. The background check law could be changed so that the gun could not be sold until the background check was complete, regardless of how long that took, but Congress would have to amend federal law. Senator Richard Blumenthal of Connecticut has proposed doing this. In October 2017, four days after the Las Vegas Strip mass shooting, Blumenthal introduced the Background Check

Completion Act of 2017. It reads, "This bill amends the federal criminal code to prohibit a licensed gun dealer from transferring a firearm to an unlicensed person prior to completion of a background check."[50]

In March 2018 the Senate Judiciary Committee held hearings on the bill—the first step toward passage. Referring to the approximately three hundred thousand potential buyers who slip through the cracks in the background check system each year, Blumenthal declared, "These numbers are especially alarming given a gaping loophole in current law that allows dangerous individuals like Charleston mass shooter Dylann Roof to legally purchase firearms if a background check isn't completed within 72 hours. . . . No check, no sale must be the rule."[51]

Raising the Age Limit

When MSD shooter Nikolas Cruz purchased the AR-15-style rifle he used in the shooting, he was nineteen years old. At the time, Florida law prohibited sales of handguns to people under twenty-one, but the age limit for buying a rifle, or long gun, was just eighteen. Cruz passed his background check and purchased the gun legally. After the Parkland shooting, the Florida legislature raised the age limit for purchasing long guns to twenty-one. Only two other states—Hawaii and Illinois—also limit the sales of long guns to those who are twenty-one, but similar bills have been introduced in California and other states. Under federal law a person has to be twenty-one to buy a handgun from a licensed dealer, but the age limit drops to eighteen if the gun is purchased from a private seller. Fifteen states have made twenty-one the age limit for purchasing any handgun, even from private sellers. The minimum age to purchase a long gun from a licensed dealer is eighteen under federal law, but there is no minimum age to purchase a long gun from an unlicensed seller.

In the aftermath of the Parkland shooting, many people are calling for a federal law to raise the age limit to twenty-one for all

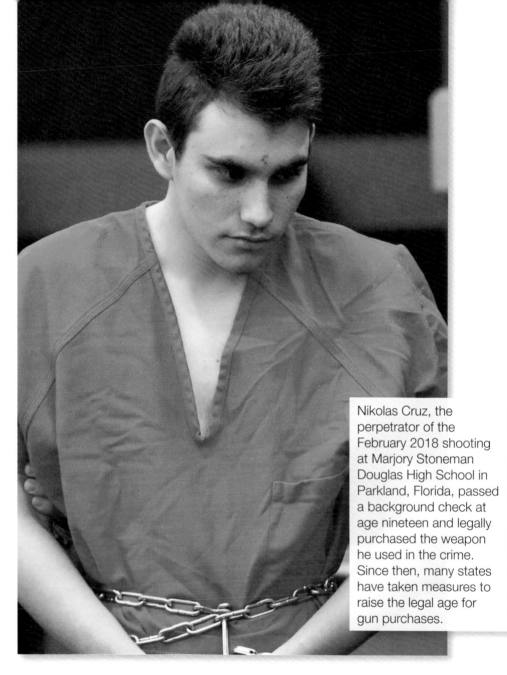

Nikolas Cruz, the perpetrator of the February 2018 shooting at Marjory Stoneman Douglas High School in Parkland, Florida, passed a background check at age nineteen and legally purchased the weapon he used in the crime. Since then, many states have taken measures to raise the legal age for gun purchases.

gun purchases. The editorial staff of the *Eagle Eye*, the MSD student newspaper, writes:

> In a few months from now, many of us will be turning 18.
> We will not be able to drink; we will not be able to rent a
> car. Most of us will still be living with our parents. We will

not be able to purchase a handgun. And yet, we will be able to purchase an AR-15. . . . That is unacceptable. It makes no sense that to buy a handgun, you have to be 21, but a gun of mass destruction and devastation like the AR-15 can be purchased when one is just becoming an adult. With the exception of those who are serving the United States in the military, the age to obtain any firearm must be raised to 21.[52]

Critics of raising the age limit for gun purchases point out that some teenaged mass shooters used guns owned by older family members or obtained the weapons from illegal sources. Similarly, they argue, banning assault weapons, tightening background checks, and outlawing high-capacity magazines would not have prevented all mass shootings or gun violence. Gun control advocates counter that a multi-pronged approach may not eliminate shootings, but it will decrease the number of gun deaths. Whether one, some, or all of the gun law proposals are adopted, millions of Americans believe the time has come to take some kind of action to reduce gun violence.

Chapter Four

An Armed Citizenry

On March 20, 2018, about one month after the Parkland shooting, Austin Wyatt Rollins, a seventeen-year-old student at Great Mills High School in southern Maryland, parked his car in the school parking lot and entered the campus carrying his father's Glock 9-millimeter pistol. Rollins approached his ex-girlfriend, sixteen-year-old Jaelynn Willey, raised the gun, and fired. The bullet struck Willey in the head. Rollins kept walking, turned a corner, and was confronted by school resource officer Blaine Gaskill. Gaskill fired at Rollins, hitting him in the hand. Rollins turned his gun on himself and ended his life. Less than a minute had elapsed from the time Rollins had first fired his weapon.

Using a Gun to Stop a Shooter

St. Mary's County sheriff Tim Cameron praised Gaskill, who serves as a SWAT team member on Cameron's force. "He responded exactly how we train our personnel to respond,"[53] Cameron told reporters. "The premise is simple: You go to the sound of gunfire."[54] Maryland governor Larry Hogan also commended Gaskill. "This is a tough guy who apparently closed in very quickly and took the right kind of action," Hogan said. "And while I think it's still tragic, he may have saved other people's lives."[55]

Coming between the nationwide school walkout to protest gun violence on March 14 and the nationwide March for Our Lives on March 24, Gaskill's actions took on national significance. He was praised by gun rights supporters not only as an outstanding school resource officer but as an example of the most effective way to deal with public shootings of all kinds:

A school resource officer shot a student who had just shot a classmate at Great Mills High School (pictured) in Great Mills, Maryland, in March 2018. Gun advocates say this demonstrates that lawfully arming school personnel will make schools safer.

using a gun. "I wonder if the #MarchForOurLives protestors will take a moment to honor the armed guard who prevented a mass shooting this week in Maryland?" asked Charlie Kirk, founder and executive director of conservative nonprofit organization Turning Point USA. "This week a gun and lawful gun owner prevented another Columbine, Parkland, and Sandy Hook. Will they even mention him?"[56]

Gaskill's actions and the training behind them grew out of law enforcement experience. "History shows when a suspect is confronted by any armed individual (police, security, concealed carry person) they either shoot it out with that person or kill themselves," state the Broward County, Florida, Sheriff's Office training and operation materials. "Either way, the shooting of innocent bystanders must stop." These materials are similar to the ones used to train Gaskill and countless other officers across the country. "If you are on scene or in the area and hear gunshots, you should immediately access what you have and prepare to respond. Remember, every time you hear a gunshot in an active shooter incident; you have to believe that is another victim being killed,"[57] instruct the materials.

> "This week a gun and lawful gun owner prevented another Columbine, Parkland, and Sandy Hook."[56]
>
> —Charlie Kirk, founder and executive director of Turning Point USA

A Tragic Failure

MSD is located in Broward County, Florida. The Broward County Sheriff's Office revealed that armed school resource officer Deputy Scot Peterson was on the scene of the MSD mass shooting, but he did not enter the school to confront shooter Nikolas Cruz. The watchdog group Judicial Watch obtained the sheriff's department training materials because it wanted to see whether Peterson had followed department procedures, as he claimed in a statement after the shooting. "The first officer or two officers on scene will immediately go to confront the shooter,"[58] state the materials, contradicting Peterson's claim.

Broward County sheriff Scott Israel admitted during a news conference that Peterson did not do what he was supposed to. Israel explained what Peterson should have done: "Went in. Addressed the killer. Killed the killer."[59] MSD student Kai Koerber lamented Peterson's failure to use force to stop the shooter. "Had our resource officer taken action immediately, the result of the Stoneman Douglas Valentine's Day Massacre would have been different," Koerber told CNN. "We might not have had to walk over the bodies of our classmates, once lovely and wonderful people, as we were led

> "Had our resource officer taken action immediately, the result of the Stoneman Douglas Valentine's Day Massacre would have been different."[60]
>
> —Kai Koerber, student at MSD

away from murderous tragedy."[60] Andrew Pollack, whose eighteen-year-old daughter, Meadow, died in the shooting, said that the officer's failure to act was "unbelievable." He wrote on Facebook, "Scot Peterson had ample enough to time to make it to the third floor and prevent 6 deaths including the death of my daughter Meadow."[61]

More Armed Guards

In the aftermath of the Parkland shooting, the Florida legislature passed, and Governor Rick Scott signed, a bill that set aside funding for more armed police officers on school campuses. "I'm not into banning specific weapons," Scott told *Fox News Sunday*. "I want to make sure we have significant law enforcement presence at schools."[62] Pollack, who also was interviewed on the program, agreed. "I just had to listen to you and Gov. Scott talk about gun control," Pollack told news anchor Chris Wallace. "We don't care about gun control right now," said Pollack. "It's not about guns now. It's about the safety of our schools."[63]

The idea of stopping school shooters with armed guards is not new. After the 2012 massacre at Sandy Hook Elementary School that left twenty-six dead and two wounded, Wayne LaPierre, the executive vice president of the NRA, said:

> You know, five years ago, after the Virginia Tech tragedy, when I said we should put armed security in every school, the media called me crazy. But what if, when Adam Lanza started shooting his way into Sandy Hook Elementary School last Friday, he had been confronted by qualified, armed security? Will you at least admit it's possible that 26 innocent lives might have been spared? . . . The only thing that stops a bad guy with a gun is a good guy with a gun. Would you rather have your 911 call bring a good guy with a gun from a mile away . . . or a minute away?[64]

The Case for Self-Protection

The vast majority of gun owners say they purchased the weapons to protect themselves. In this excerpt, attorney and journalist David French explains why he and his wife choose to have guns.

It starts with the consciousness of a threat. Perhaps not the kind of threat my family has experienced. Some people experience more. Some less. And some people don't experience a threat at all—but they're aware of those who do. With the consciousness of a threat comes the awareness of a vulnerability. The police can only protect the people you love in the most limited of circumstances (with those limits growing ever-more-severe the farther you live from a city center.) . . .

Yes, if someone tried to break into your house, you know that you'd call 911 and pray for the police to come quickly, but you also start to think of exactly what else you'd do. If you heard that "bump" in the night, how would you protect yourself until the police arrived? . . .

Because of the threats against my family—and because I don't want to be dependent on a sometimes shockingly incompetent government for my family's security—I carry a weapon. My wife does as well. We're not scared. We're prepared, and that sense of preparation is contagious. Confidence is contagious. People want to be empowered. That's how gun culture is built. Not by the NRA and not by Congress, but by gun owners, one free citizen at a time.

David French, "What Critics Don't Understand About Gun Culture," *Atlantic*, February 27, 2018. www.theatlantic.com.

Those who support the use of guns to stop shooters often point to the hypocrisy of those who disagree with the policy but are themselves protected by armed guards. "Members of Congress work in offices surrounded by armed Capitol Police officers," said LaPierre. "Yet when it comes to the most beloved, innocent and vulnerable members of the American family—our children—we as a society leave them utterly defenseless."[65]

Gun owners march in Idaho to support a 2016 law that allows citizens to carry concealed weapons without a permit. Supporters of such laws say they are needed so that citizens can defend themselves rather than having to wait for law enforcement officers to arrive when a crime is in progress.

Self-Protection

The argument that another individual with a gun is the only way to stop a bad guy with a gun is used to support not only more armed guards but also an armed citizenry. Gun rights advocates do not think people confronted with a gun should have to hope that a good guy gets there fast enough. Many firearm owners carry a gun so they do not have to wait for help. The reason all fifty states allow concealed carry—and a growing number are allowing it without a permit—is that the leaders in those states believe people should be able to defend themselves. According to the Crime Prevention Research Center, concealed carry permits issued by state and local governments increased by 215 percent from 2007 through 2015, to more than 14 million Americans. More than 6 percent of the US adult population has a concealed carry permit. "The formula is simple: Criminals and the dangerously mentally ill make our nation more violent," writes attorney and journalist David French. "Law-abiding gun owners save and protect lives."[66]

Critics of permitless concealed carry believe an armed citizenry poses a danger greater than the ill it is meant to cure. Many states require gun owners to pass a safety test before receiving a concealed carry permit. In states that do not require a permit, gun owners do not have to prove they can handle a gun safely before carrying a concealed weapon. Before the lower house of the North Carolina state legislature passed a law to allow permitless concealed carry in 2017, Peter Ambler, executive director of Americans for Responsible Solutions, a gun control advocacy organization, argued against the bill when it went before the state senate. "You don't want folks carrying around an incredibly dangerous consumer product like a firearm without knowing how to use it,"[67] Ambler said. The gun control lobbying group North Carolinians Against Gun Violence agreed, saying, "Make no mistake, permitless carry puts everyone in the community at risk, significantly weakens law enforcement's ability to protect the public, and threatens citizens' rights to safely and peaceably enjoy public spaces in their community."[68] Explaining why the state of Hawaii opposed a federal law that would require states to allow visitors from permitless carry states to bring their weapons into other states, Hawaii's attorney general, Doug Chin, said, "Hawaii lawmakers already made decisions about firearms and public safety that best serve our state. We will resist any efforts by the federal government to turn our state into the Wild West."[69]

> "The formula is simple: Criminals and the dangerously mentally ill make our nation more violent. Law-abiding gun owners save and protect lives."[66]
>
> —David French, attorney and journalist

The Effects of Concealed Carry

The findings of research on the effects of right-to-carry (RTC) laws are mixed. A 2017 study led by John J. Donohue of Stanford University used computer modeling to simulate the effect of RTC laws. Rather than comparing raw numbers from RTC and non-RTC states, Donohue's team estimated what would have happened in RTC states if they had not adopted RTC laws, on the basis of trends from other states. "Ten years after the adoption of RTC laws, violent crime is estimated to be 13–15 percent higher than it would have been without the RTC law,"[70] writes Donohue. However, critics question Donohue's methodology. They believe he overused Hawaii as a standard of comparison. "In the cases of Idaho and Minnesota, over 96 percent of the comparison is just with Hawaii," writes researcher John R. Lott, author of *More Guns, Less Crime*. "For Mississippi, Nebraska, and Utah, Hawaii counts for between 72 percent and 83 percent of the comparison."[71]

Lott's own 2016 study came to vastly different conclusions. His team found that in 2014 the seven states that allowed concealed carry without a permit had lower rates of murder and violent crime than did the seven states with the lowest percentage of permit holders. The researchers found that the violent crime rate was 28 percent lower in RTC states and the murder rate 31 percent lower. Such raw numbers ignore the vast differences between states. For example, some of the states with the lowest permit rates, such as Illinois and Maryland, are home to cities with high crime rates. Many of the permitless states have largely rural areas, where crime rates are low. Accordingly, Lott and his team also looked at murder rates only in states that require permits. They found that the more concealed carry permit carriers a state has, the lower its murder rate is. "State level permit data suggests that each one percentage point increase in the percent of the adult population holding permits is roughly associated with a 25 percent drop in the murder rate,"[72] write the researchers. However, like many other gun studies, Lott's findings did not show a causal link; that is, they do not show that more permit carriers caused the lower murder rates.

Is *Gun* a Bad Word?

After the shooting at Sandy Hook Elementary School, Wayne LaPierre, executive director of the NRA, held a press conference to call on Congress to pass a law putting armed police officers in every school. In this excerpt, LaPierre addresses members of the press attending the event.

I can imagine the shocking headlines you'll print tomorrow morning: "More guns," you'll claim, "are the NRA's answer to everything!" Your implication will be that guns are evil and have no place in society, much less in our schools. But since when did the word "gun" automatically become a bad word?

A gun in the hands of a Secret Service agent protecting the President isn't a bad word. A gun in the hands of a soldier protecting the United States isn't a bad word. And when you hear the glass breaking in your living room at 3 a.m. and call 911, you won't be able to pray hard enough for a gun in the hands of a good guy to get there fast enough to protect you.

So why is the idea of a gun good when it's used to protect our President or our country or our police, but bad when it's used to protect our children in their schools?

They're our kids. They're our responsibility. And it's not just our duty to protect them—it's our right to protect them.

Wayne LaPierre, "NRA: Full Statement by Wayne LaPierre in Response to Newtown Shootings," *Guardian* (Manchester), December 21, 2012. www.theguardian.com.

A Law-Abiding Group

The Crime Prevention Research Center found that concealed carry permit holders commit fewer crimes than the general population. The conviction rates of concealed carry permit holders are more than two hundred times lower than the conviction rate of the US population as a whole. Concealed carry permit holders even commit fewer crimes than off-duty police officers, according to the study. "We find that permit holders are convicted of misdemeanors and felonies at less than a sixth the rate for police officers," states the group's report. "Indeed, it is impossible to think of any other group in the US that is anywhere near as law-abiding."[73] The fact that concealed carry permit holders are a low risk for committing crimes, including gun-related crimes suggests that arming them is not as great a danger as critics suggest. "With 16 million permit holders across 50 states, it is telling that not one state has ever held a legislative hearing to consider rescinding right-to-carry laws,"[74] writes Lott.

As the number of gun owners has surged, so has the number of people who believe that guns make them safer. A 2000 Gallup poll found that just 35 percent of Americans thought that owning a gun made their home safer, but by 2014 that number had grown to 63 percent. Two polls by the Pew Research Center found the same result. A 2012 poll found that 48 percent of the respondents said they believe owning a gun would protect them against crime, as opposed to 37 percent who said that owning a gun would put their safety at risk. Just two years later, in 2014, those who had the positive impression of guns had grown to 57 percent. A 2017 poll by the Pew Research Center found that 67 percent of gun owners cite protection as a major reason for owning a gun.

Critics of the self-defense theory of gun ownership paint a different picture. "From a personal-safety standpoint, more guns means less safety," writes New York Times columnist Bret Stephens. "The F.B.I. counted a total of 268 'justifiable homicides' by private citizens involving firearms in 2015; that is, felons killed in the course of committing a felony. Yet that same year, there were 489 'unintentional firearms deaths' in the United States, according to the Centers for Disease Control."[75] The rarity of defensive-gun-use (DGU) deaths is not surprising, since killings are far rarer than other DGU incidents, such as wounding an assailant or deterring a would-be criminal by brandishing a gun. According to a study by Florida State University criminologists Gary Kleck and Marc Gertz, 76 percent of DGUs did not involve firing the weapon.

Counting Defensive Gun Uses

Determining the exact number of DGUs is extremely difficult. In their study, the National Self-Defense Survey (NSDS), Kleck and Gertz interviewed five thousand gun owners. The researchers asked the respondents if they had used a gun for self-protection or protection at any time in the past five years. Those who said yes were then asked what Kleck describes as a "detailed series of questions establishing exactly what happened," including the "specific crime they thought was being committed."[76] This helped the researchers determine whether the DGUs actually occurred. Kleck and Getz found 222 bona fide DGUs via the survey. The researchers used the sampling to estimate that 2.2 million to 2.5 million DGUs happen in the United States each year.

Other researchers have come to vastly different conclusions. The National Crime Victimization Survey, conducted in 1998 by the US Census Bureau on behalf of the US Department of Justice, found just 116,000 DGUs per year—95 percent fewer than the NSDS survey result. However, as the name of the survey suggests, it gathered data only from crime victims, not all gun owners. In addition, the victims were asked whether they did or attempted to do something about the crime while it was happening, not whether they used a gun. It is possible that some respondents were reluctant to tell a government official about actions they took with a firearm. A 2014 study by the Gun Violence Archive found just 1,581 DGUs per year. These researchers said they derived their count from 1,200 media sources, police blotters, and police media outlets. In other words, the researchers counted only DGUs reported to the police or the media. However, the vast majority of DGUs that do not result in death or injury are not reported to the police.

For many gun owners, the number of DGUs is irrelevant. Brian Doherty, a senior editor at *Reason* magazine and author of *Gun Control on Trial*, writes:

> Those people who lived out . . . DGUs would doubtless find it curious to hear they shouldn't have had the right to defend themselves, because an insufficiently impressive number of other citizens had done the same. . . . However large the number of DGUs, or how small; and however large the number of accidents or tragedies caused by guns, or how small, the right and ability to choose for yourself how to defend yourself and your family—at home or away from it—remains, and that numerical debate should have no particular bearing on it.[77]

The Right to Self-Preservation

For the 100 million US gun owners and the millions more who support them, self-defense is a right—the most important right of all, since no other rights can be enjoyed if a person is deprived of his or her life. "I should have a right to destroy that which threatens me with destruction,"[78] wrote British philosopher John Locke one hundred years before the US Constitution was ratified.

A decade before the American Revolution, British legal scholar William Blackstone wrote that the right to bear arms was linked to the right of self-preservation. "Having arms for their defence . . . is indeed a public allowance, under due restrictions, of the natural right of resistance and self-preservation, when the sanctions of society and laws are found insufficient to restrain the violence of oppression."[79] Certainly it is better to rely on the laws and police for protection, but when society's protections are insufficient, American law—and the British law on which it was based—allow for the basic right of self-defense.

While gun control advocates argue that people should rely on laws and police for protection, gun rights advocates say that gun ownership is inseparable from the right to protect oneself. Indeed, both American law and the British law from which it was derived allow for the basic right of self-defense.

Disarmament or Deterrence

The inability of the police to be everywhere at all times leaves American society with two alternatives for protection against gun violence: allowing those who feel confident to arm themselves or banning guns altogether. As a *Stanford Review* blogger going only by the name seck writes:

> In theory, the left's position on gun control would be optimal ("No Guns, No Crime"). In practice, however, the right's position ("More Guns, Less Crime") makes sense in the absence of an existing federal gun-control policy that is 100% effective. Either of these solutions would work. Unfortunately, a mixed, decentralized stance on this particular issue would not, given the unique power and danger held by those who hold guns.[80]

Seck points out that the tiny nation of Singapore has banned citizens from owning guns, and its soldiers are not allowed to take their guns home. As a result, Singapore has the lowest crime rate in the developed world. "We will require a total ban on civilian ownership of guns because if our gun-control laws are rigorous, but not absolute, the vast majority of innocent people will be completely defenseless against the few criminals who manage to procure guns," seck continues. If a total ban is not possible, seck argues, individuals must be free to defend themselves. Seck explains, "Gun control is one of those rare issues where extreme solutions, not compromises, are needed. Disarmament would work. Deterrence would work. But anything in between will not."[81] It remains to be seen which path America will take.

Source Notes

Introduction: Parkland and Beyond

1. Quoted in David Fleshler and Yiran Zhu, "Timeline: How the Stoneman Douglas High School Shooting Unfolded," *Sun Sentinel* (Broward County, FL), March 9, 2018. www.sun -sentinel.com.

2. Nicholas Kristof, "Lessons from the Virginia Shooting," *New York Times*, August 26, 2015. www.nytimes.com.

3. Kathy Durham, "Opinion: A Student's Obituary Should Never Say 'Gunned Down While Studying for Chemistry,'" PBS, February 16, 2018. www.pbs.org.

4. Quoted in *Face the Nation*, "Transcript: Florida School Shooting Survivors on *Face the Nation*, Feb. 18, 2018," CBS News, February 18, 2018. www.cbsnews.com.

5. Quoted in Colleen Shalby, "Members of the First Generation to Grow Up with Social Media at Its Fingertips Launch a Gun-Control Movement," *Los Angeles Times*, February 23, 2018. www.latimes.com.

6. March for Our Lives, Twitter, February 2018. https://twitter .com.

7. Quoted in Julie Turkewitz et al., "A Parkland Student Steps Up, and Her Voice Is Heard When She Says to Politicians, 'We Call BS!,'" *Boston Globe*, February 18, 2018. www.bos tonglobe.com.

8. Quoted in Ray Sanchez and Holly Yan, "Florida Gov. Rick Scott Signs Gun Bill," CNN, March 10, 2018. https://edition .cnn.com.

9. Ted Deutch, Twitter, March 7, 2018. https://twitter.com.

Chapter One: A Uniquely American Problem

10. Thomas Jefferson, "Letter to William S. Smith, 1787," James Madison Research Library and Information Center. www .madisonbrigade.com.

11. Richard Henry Lee, "Letters from the Federal Farmer to the Republican," James Madison Research Library and Information Center. www.madisonbrigade.com.

12. George Washington, "To the United States Senate and House of Representatives," Papers of George Washington Digital Edition, University of Virginia Press. http://rotunda.upress .virginia.edu.

13. James Lindgren and Justin L. Heather, "Counting Guns in Early America," *William & Mary Law Review*, 2002. http:// scholarship.law.wm.edu.

14. Charles M. Blow, "America Is the Gun," *New York Times*, February 25, 2018. www.nytimes.com.

15. Quoted in Nurith Aizenman, "Gun Violence: How the U.S. Compares with Other Countries," *Goats and Soda* (blog), NPR, October 6, 2017. www.npr.org.

16. Lane Kenworthy, "Guns," *The Good Society* (blog), November 2017. https://lanekenworthy.net.

17. Quoted in Cydney Hargis, "NRA's News Outlet Says It's 'Fake News' to Say There Are over 30,000 U.S. Gun Deaths Each Year Because the Figure Includes Gun Suicides," Media Matters for America, January 8, 2018. www.mediamatters.org.

18. Hargis, "NRA's News Outlet Says It's 'Fake News' to Say There Are over 30,000 U.S. Gun Deaths Each Year Because the Figure Includes Gun Suicides."

19. Quoted in Rachel Ehrenberg, "What We Do and Don't Know About How to Prevent Gun Violence," *Science News*, March 9, 2018. www.sciencenews.org.

20. Quoted in Beth Duff-Brow, "Gun Violence and Suicide by Firearm Is a Public Health Epidemic," Stanford University, March 16, 2017. http://fsi.stanford.edu.

21. Andrew R. Morral et al., *The Science of Gun Policy: A Critical Synthesis of Research Evidence on the Effects of Gun Policies in the United States*. Santa Monica, CA: Rand Corporation, 2018, p. 333. www.rand.org.

22. Carly Novell, Twitter, March 2, 2018. https://twitter.com.

Chapter Two: A Patchwork of Laws

23. New State Ice Co. v. Liebmann, 285 U.S. 262 (1932). Justia. https://supreme.justia.com.
24. District of Columbia v. Heller, 554 U.S. 570 (2008). Justia. https://supreme.justia.com.
25. District of Columbia v. Heller.
26. District of Columbia v. Heller.
27. District of Columbia v. Heller.
28. United States v. Miller, 307 U.S. 174 (1939). Justia. https://supreme.justia.com.
29. District of Columbia v. Heller.
30. Quoted in Tim Dickinson, "The Assault Weapons Ban the NRA Couldn't Stop," *Rolling Stone*, December 9, 2015. www.rollingstone.com.
31. Friedman v. City of Highland Park, No. 14-3091 (7th Cir. 2015). Justia. https://law.justia.com.
32. Arie S. Friedman, et al. v. City of Highland Park, Illinois, 577 U.S. (2015). www.supremecourt.gov.
33. Quoted in Dickinson, "The Assault Weapons Ban the NRA Couldn't Stop."

Chapter Three: Strengthening Gun Laws

34. Bret Stephens, "Repeal the Second Amendment," *New York Times*, October 5, 2017. www.nytimes.com.
35. March for Our Lives, "An Act to Protect & Save Your Children," 2018. https://marchforourlives.com.
36. Quoted in US Department of Justice, "Attorney General Sessions Announces Regulation Effectively Banning Bump Stocks," March 23, 2018. www.justice.gov.
37. Quoted in Robert Farley, "Did the 1994 Assault Weapons Ban Work?," FactCheck.org, February 1, 2013. www.factcheck.org.
38. Quoted in Farley, "Did the 1994 Assault Weapons Ban Work?"
39. Quoted in Farley, "Did the 1994 Assault Weapons Ban Work?"
40. S. Chapman et al., "Australia's 1996 Gun Law Reforms: Faster Falls in Firearm Deaths, Firearm Suicides, and a Decade

Without Mass Shootings," *Injury Prevention*, 2006. http://in juryprevention.bmj.com.

41. Wang-Sheng Lee and Sandy Suardi, "The Australian Firearms Buyback and Its Effect on Gun Deaths," *Contemporary Economic Policy*, January 22, 2010, p. 69. http://ro.uow.edu.au.

42. David Hemenway and Mary Vriniotis. "The Australian Gun Buyback," *Bullet-Ins*, Spring 2011. https://cdn1.sph.harvard .edu.

43. Assault Weapons Ban of 2018, H.R. 5087, 115th Congress (2017–2018). Congress.gov. www.congress.gov.

44. Quoted in Kaitlyn Schallhorn, "Gun Control Measures Proposed by Trump, Lawmakers After Florida School Shooting," Fox News, March 16, 2018. www.foxnews.com.

45. Bureau of Alcohol, Tobacco, Firearms and Explosives, "Do I Need a License To Buy and Sell Firearms?," January 2016. www.atf.gov.

46. March for Our Lives, "An Act to Protect & Save Your Children."

47. Nicholas J. Johnson, "Imagining Gun Control in America: Understanding the Remainder Problem," *Wake Forest Law Review*, 2008. https://ir.lawnet.fordham.edu.

48. Quoted in Amy Sherman, "PolitiFact Sheet: 3 Things to Know About the 'Gun Show Loophole,'" PolitiFact, January 7, 2016. www.politifact.com.

49. Johnson, "Imagining Gun Control in America."

50. Background Check Completion Act of 2017, 115th Congress (2017–2018). Congress.gov. www.congress.gov.

51. Quoted in Joshua Eaton, "Exclusive: New Data on the Massive Background Check Loophole the NRA Doesn't Want to Fix," ThinkProgress, February 27, 2018. https://thinkprogress.org.

52. Editorial staff of the *Eagle Eye*, "Our Manifesto to Fix America's Gun Laws," *Guardian* (Manchester), March 23, 2018. www .theguardian.com.

Chapter Four: An Armed Citizenry

53. Quoted in Carma Hassan and Saeed Ahmed, "Lone Resource Officer's Quick Action Stopped the Maryland School Shooter Within Seconds," CNN, March 21, 2018. https://edition.cnn .com.

54. Quoted in Matthew Barakat and Jesse J. Holland, "Teen Shoots Girl in Maryland School, Killed in Confrontation," *New London (CT) Day*, March 21, 2018. www.theday.com.

55. Quoted in Hassan and Ahmed, "Lone Resource Officer's Quick Action Stopped the Maryland School Shooter Within Seconds."

56. Charlie Kirk, Twitter, March 24, 2018. https://twitter.com.

57. Quoted in Judicial Watch, "Broward County Sheriff's Office Training Materials Say First One or Two Officers on Scene Should 'Confront the Shooter,'" March 15, 2018. www.judicialwatch.org.

58. Quoted in Judicial Watch, "Broward County Sheriff's Office Training Materials Say First One or Two Officers on Scene Should 'Confront the Shooter.'"

59. Quoted in Judicial Watch, "Broward County Sheriff's Office Training Materials Say First One or Two Officers on Scene Should 'Confront the Shooter.'"

60. Quoted in Hassan and Ahmed, "Lone Resource Officer's Quick Action Stopped the Maryland School Shooter Within Seconds."

61. Quoted in Larry McShane, "Dad Slams Parkland School Officer for Waiting Outside While Shooter Killed His Daughter," *New York Daily News*, February 24, 2018. www.nydailynews.com.

62. Quoted in Marisa Schultz, "Rick Scott Rejects Trump's Pitch to Arm Teachers," *New York Daily News*, February 25, 2018. https://nypost.com.

63. Quoted in Schultz, "Rick Scott Rejects Trump's Pitch to Arm Teachers."

64. Wayne LaPierre, "NRA: Full Statement by Wayne LaPierre in Response to Newtown Shootings," *Guardian* (Manchester), December 21, 2012. www.theguardian.com.

65. LaPierre, "NRA."

66. David French, "What Critics Don't Understand About Gun Culture," *Atlantic*, February 27, 2018. www.theatlantic.com.

67. Quoted in Craig Jarvis, "The NRA Is Pushing to Eliminate Concealed Carry Permits in NC and Across the Country," *Raleigh (NC) News & Observer*, June 20, 2017. www.newsobserver.com.

68. Quoted in Rob Schofield, "Editorial: Senate Should Bury Reckless Concealed Carry Bill," *Progressive Pulse* (blog), NC Policy Watch, June 12, 2017. http://pulse.ncpolicywatch .org.

69. Quoted in Governor of the State of Hawai'i David Y. Ige, "ATG News Release: Hawaii Opposes Forced Concealed Carry Reciprocity," news release, October 23, 2017. https://gover nor.hawaii.gov.

70. John J. Donohue et al., "Right-to-Carry Laws and Violent Crime: A Comprehensive Assessment Using Panel Data, the LASSO, and a State-Level Synthetic Controls Analysis," National Bureau of Economic Research, January 2018. www .nber.org.

71. John R. Lott, "Stanford Law Prof Gets It Wrong on Guns—Right-to-Carry Reduces Crime, Not the Other Way Around," Fox News, July 10, 2017. www.foxnews.com.

72. Crime Prevention Research Center, "Concealed Carry Permit Holders Across the United States: 2016," July 26, 2016. https://ssrn.com.

73. Crime Prevention Research Center, "Concealed Carry Permit Holders Across the United States."

74. Lott, "Stanford Law Prof Gets It Wrong on Guns."

75. Stephens, "Repeal the Second Amendment."

76. Quoted in Brian Doherty, "How to Count the Defensive Use of Guns," *Hit & Run* (blog), *Reason*, March 9, 2015. http:// reason.com.

77. Doherty, "How to Count the Defensive Use of Guns."

78. John Locke, *The Second Treatise of Government* (1690). Project Gutenberg, July 28, 2010. www.gutenberg.org.

79. William Blackstone, *Commentaries on the Laws of England*, 1765. http://press-pubs.uchicago.edu.

80. Seck, "All or Nothing," *Stanford Review*, 2007. https://stan fordreview.org.

81. Seck, "All or Nothing."

Organizations and Websites

American Public Health Association

www.apha.org

A nonprofit organization, the American Public Health Association speaks out on public health issues and policies. The gun violence area of the website provides articles, fact sheets, research and data, news, useful links, and other resources.

Brady Campaign to Prevent Gun Violence

840 First St. NE, Suite 400
Washington, DC 20002
www.bradycampaign.org

Founded in 1974 as the National Council to Control Handguns, the Brady Campaign to Prevent Gun Violence was renamed in 2001 in honor of James Brady and his wife, Sarah. The organization has a goal of cutting the number of US gun deaths in half by 2025 through stronger background checks, cracking down on irresponsible gun dealers, and educating the public about gun violence.

Coalition to Stop Gun Violence (CSGV)

805 Fifteenth St. NW
Washington, DC 20005
www.csgv.org

The CSGV is a nonprofit organization founded in 1974 with the goal of building communities free from gun violence. The organization pursues this goal through research, policy development, and lobbying for gun control legislation.

Everytown for Gun Safety

450 Lexington Ave.
New York, NY 10022
www.everytown.org

Founded in 2014 by former New York City mayor Michael Bloomberg, Everytown for Gun Safety is a nonprofit organization that advocates for gun control and against gun violence. With a membership surpassing 4 million, it has successfully lobbied for gun control legislation at the local and state levels.

Giffords Law Center to Prevent Gun Violence

http://lawcenter.giffords.org

A nonprofit organization with a mission to save lives from gun violence, the center provides a wealth of legal information on areas such as the Second Amendment, background checks, guns in public, gun owner responsibilities, and more. Its website features information about the laws of each state as well as federal laws.

GunPolicy.Org

www.gunpolicy.org

This website presents research from the University of Sydney in Australia. One page features an interactive chart maker that allows the user to compare gun death rates per one hundred thousand people for any mix of countries and instantly see a bar graph illustrating the comparisons.

Gun Violence Archive

www.gunviolencearchive.org

This not-for-profit organization provides free online public access to accurate information about gun-related violence in the United States. Its home page keeps a list of gun-related incidents for the year, updated hourly. The list includes number of incidents, deaths, injuries, children and teens killed or injured, home invasions, and more.

Marshall Project

156 W. Fifty-Sixth St., Suite 701
New York, NY 10019
www.themarshallproject.org

The Marshall Project is a nonpartisan, nonprofit news organization that seeks to create and sustain a sense of national urgency about the US criminal justice system. The website includes a mass shooting page that links to dozens of web pages with information on mass shootings and gun control.

National Rifle Association (NRA)

11250 Waples Mill Rd.
Fairfax, VA 22030
https://home.nra.org

Founded in 1871, the NRA is a nonprofit organization that advocates for Second Amendment rights. The organization has about 5 million members and lobbies for the rights of gun owners.

The Trace

www.thetrace.org

The Trace is a nonprofit newsroom covering gun violence in America. The website includes a daily roundup of news stories on gun violence and gun control legislation. It features an interactive map plotting the locations of nearly forty thousand incidents of gun violence nationwide.

For Further Research

Books

John Allen, *Thinking Critically: Gun Control*. San Diego: Reference-Point, 2018.

Anne Cunningham, *Guns: Conceal and Carry*. New York: Greenhaven, 2018.

Adam Furgang, *Everything You Need to Know About Gun Violence*. New York: Rosen, 2018.

Carol Hand, *Gun Control and the Second Amendment*. Minneapolis: Essential Library, 2017.

Bridget Heing, *Investigating Mass Shootings in the United States*. New York: Rosen, 2018.

John R. Lott Jr., *The War on Guns: Arming Yourself Against Gun Control Lies*. Washington, DC: Regnery, 2016.

Internet Sources

Mark Abadi, "The 12 Deadliest Mass Shootings in Modern US History," Business Insider, February 15, 2018. www.businessin sider.com/deadliest-mass-shootings-in-us-history-2017-10.

BBC, "America's Gun Culture in 10 Charts," March 21, 2018. www.bbc.com/news/world-us-canada-41488081.

Bonnie Berkowitz, Denise Lu, and Chris Alcantara, "The Terrible Numbers That Grow with Each Mass Shooting," *Washington Post*, December 14, 2012; updated April 24, 2018. www.washington post.com/graphics/2018/national/mass-shootings-in-america /?utm_term=.731d15a0f6de.

John Woodrow Cox, "Inside an Accused School Shooter's Mind: A Plot to Kill '50 or 60. If I Get Lucky Maybe 150,'" *Washington Post*, March 3, 2018. https://www.washingtonpost.com/local/ inside-a-teen-school-shooters-mind-a-plot-to-kill-50-or-60-if-i -get-lucky-maybe-150/2018/03/03/68cc673c-1b27-11e8-ae5a -16e60e4605f3_story.html.

Editorial staff of the *Eagle Eye*, "Our Manifesto to Fix America's Gun Laws," *Guardian* (Manchester), March 23, 2018. www.the guardian.com/us-news/commentisfree/2018/mar/23/parkland -students-manifesto-americas-gun-laws.

Rachel Ehrenberg, "What We Do and Don't Know About How to Prevent Gun Violence," *Science News*, March 9, 2018. www .sciencenews.org/article/evidence-preventing-gun-violence -deaths-research.

David French, "What Critics Don't Understand About Gun Culture," *Atlantic*, February 27, 2018. www.theatlantic.com/politics /archive/2018/02/gun-culture/554351.

German Lopez, "America's Unique Gun Violence Problem, Explained in 17 Maps and Charts," Vox, April 4, 2018. www.vox .com/policy-and-politics/2017/10/2/16399418/us-gun-violence -statistics-maps-charts.

Index

Picture Credits